SKILLS IN
HOME ECONOMICS
TECHNOLOGY

Jenny Ridgwell with Louise Davies

HEINEMANN
EDUCATIONAL

Heinemann Educational,
a division of **Heinemann Educational Books Ltd**,
Halley Court, Jordan Hill, Oxford OX2 8EJ

OXFORD LONDON EDINBURGH
MELBOURNE SYDNEY AUCKLAND
IBADAN NAIROBI GABORONE HARARE
KINGSTON PORTSMOUTH NH (USA)
SINGAPORE MADRID

First published 1989

British Library Cataloguing in Publication Data

Ridgwell, Jenny
  Skills in home economics: technology.
  1. Food technology
  I. Title II. Davies, Louise
  664

ISBN 0 435 42002 X

Designed and produced by
The Pen and Ink Book Company Ltd, Huntingdon, Cambridgeshire

Printed and bound in Spain by Mateu Cromo

Acknowledgements

Thanks are due to the following for permission to reproduce copyright material: Adams Foods Ltd. for the Kerrygold Light Milk label on p. 23; British Bakeries for the Windmill label on p. 26; British Gas Education Service for the illustration from the 'Homemaking with Gas' series on p. 16; The Boots Company PLC for the drink label on p. 29; H. J. Heinz Co. Ltd for the baby food label on p. 20 and the spaghetti label on p. 38; Kellogg Company of Great Britain for the illustration on p. 42; Klinge Foods Limited for the Lo Salt label on p. 23; National Air and Space Museum (Washington DC) for the ice cream label on p. 15; The Nestlé Company Ltd. for the Waistline label on p. 22; Oxfam Education for the letter (from *Potato Profile* which retails at £0.75) on p. 68; Pasta Foods Limited for the Record label on p. 39; Rowntree Limited for the jelly label on p. 60; The Ryvita Company Ltd. for the label on p. 22; Sainsburys PLC for the bread label on p. 26, the illustration on additives on p. 59 and the till receipt on p. 74.

Thanks are also due to the following for permission to reproduce photographs: Amberley Chalk Pits Museum p. 86; The Boots Company PLC p. 17; Mary Evans Picture Library p. 58; Hulton Picture Company p. 72; Leatherhead Food Research Association p. 69; Metal Box p. 71; Mothercare p. 19; Museum of English Rural Life (University of Reading) pp. 46 and 54; Oxfam p. 68; Pasta Information Centre p. 24; Rank Hovis Ltd. p. 32; Ann Ronan Picture Library p. 52; Science Photo Library p. 14; Weald and Downland Open Air Museum p. 80.
All other photographs supplied by Jenny Ridgwell.

Cover illustration by Pat Thorne.

Illustrations by Natalie Bould, Jane Cheswright, Dataset Marlborough Design, Eugene Fleury, Maureen and Gordon Gray, Dave Parkins, Martin Salisbury, John York.

Contents

Since technology can be tackled in so many ways, we have offered a range of ideas in the double page spreads. Some work may take weeks, some can be done in a single or double lesson.

For each section, we have tried to explain why the work is about **design and technology**.

Design and technology could be looked upon as a series of stages.

- **First stage** think about the *needs* or opportunities
- **Second stage** get some *ideas* by asking others or *researching*
- **Third stage** *plan* and *test out* these ideas and get some results
- **Fourth stage** now think about what you have done – *appraise* your work. This appraisal should take place throughout the **'design and making'** programme.

The spreads include some questions and answers using the text, but also much investigative research and questioning of ideas. There are many practical activities including making butter or margarine. Other activities include designing new recipes, packaging or labels.

The 'Assess yourself' page can be filled in when a section of work is completed.

Symbols show the type of work or activity for each section.

written work to be done

 needs other books for help

recipes or practical work

 investigation which involves looking carefully at something

a design and make activity

 discussion with the rest of the group

areas of work where a computer could speed things up

The authors would like to thank Sue Walton, the publisher, Annabel and Simon Ridgwell and the pupils of Aspen House School. We hope that the book encourages teachers and pupils to explore their own ideas on design and technology. This is only the very beginning!

What is design and technology?

To do

We all have different needs. Have a **brainstorming session** to find out what our needs are. Don't think of just *your needs*. What about disabled people, different age groups and people in other parts of the world?

We all have to make and change things in life to meet our needs. **Design and technology** is about providing for our **needs**.

But what are needs?

Let's think about design and technology and the **need for food**.

A needy family

What do teenagers **need** to eat? You must find out what teenagers like and need to eat by **research** or asking them for **ideas**.

The task could be to plan a day's meals for a teenager.

Think about the **constraints** – things that will affect the food you choose. One constraint could be choosing food that they like. Think of other constraints.

Now you need to **plan** and maybe **test** what you have chosen for the day's meals. You could prepare some of the food to taste. You can **appraise** your work by thinking about the problems you met and what **changes** you made.

Let's write this in simple stages.

Stages in design and technology
- The **task** – to plan a day's meals for a teenager.
- **Ideas** – do some **research** and ask people.
- **Plan** and **test** – prepare some food to taste.
- **Appraise** – think about the problems you met and how you changed things.

Design and technology is about being able to use and control the things around us to meet our **needs**. Early people needed to learn how to build shelters, make clothes and prepare food to eat. All these were different ways of using things around them to meet their needs.

When technology is about the things that we **eat**, it can be called **food technology**. Food technology has been around ever since early people learnt to gather the seeds of wild grasses or catch wild animals or fish. They discovered how to feed themselves by making the seeds into porridge or bread and by cooking the animals to make them tender and safe to eat.

'Design and technology' is about **solving** these kinds of problems and getting some **ideas** which you can **test out** and come up with a **solution**.

Then you can think about ways to **improve** what you have done.

So the Early Hairy family have been faced with some difficult **food problems**. But with the help of others they have come up with some **ideas** then **tested them out** and come up with a **solution**! But could they **improve** their solution?

These are the stages in the process of design and technology.

So let's look at the problem of eating raw meat or fish.

The problem!

This wild pig is chewy and tastes nasty.

How can we change this wild pig and make it taste better?

Sometimes there are creepy crawlies on it and it makes us feel sick.

Ideas!

The family over the hill know how to make their wild pig hot. Then it's not so tough and chewy.

Let's try out this 'fire' idea.

Test out the idea

This fire will soon give us hot wild pig.

Lovely! Now let's try hot fish, birds, porridge....

Come up with a result and think about improvements

Stages in design and technology

- Think about the **problem** or **need**.
- Get some **ideas** and **help**.
- **Test out** your ideas. Do they need **changing**?
- Come up with a **result**. Can you **improve** it?

Here are some other **problems** the Early Hairy Family need to solve:

(a) catching and cooking a fish
(b) gathering seeds to make porridge
(c) making a shelter
(d) making clothes or shoes

Work in small groups. Think about how you would solve *one* of these problems.

Tips you should remember

These people lived in the Stone Age so they had no saucepans, knives or spoons, scissors, metal axes and needles or rope. These are known as **constraints**.

They did have sticks, bones, hair and skin from animals, sharp stone flint to make cutting tools, clay for pottery.

Simon's group decided to think about the **problem–'gathering seeds to make porridge'**.
They talked about **ideas** for:
- how to make pots to carry things in
- how to get clean water to use for cooking
- how to grind the seeds

They wrote down their **solutions** and then told the rest of the class.

1 In your group follow these stages in design and technology.
- Write down the **problem** or **need.**
- Talk about some **ideas.**
- How would you **solve the problem** if you lived in the Stone Age?
- What **improvements** could you make?

Now, present your work to the rest of the class. Ask them for their views on how you could improve on what you have done.

2 These early people began to develop their ideas on technology to produce other things.

Working in small groups, design a task which could be carried out by Stone Age people. Work through the stages in design and technology for this task. Think about the **constraints** (what things can't you use or do?). Present your work to the rest of the class and ask them for their views on your ideas.

Some new foods are discovered by accident

In the past, many new foods were discovered by accident. Imagine that you were making some biscuits from flour and water and you forgot about them for a day. The mixture would expand in size and when you cooked it you would have discovered how to make bread!

Designing new foods

Nowadays a team of many people is needed to design and make a new food to sell in the shops. The flow diagram shows the team of people needed to design and make a new breakfast cereal.

Designing a new breakfast cereal

Scientists investigate packing materials, work out the 'shelf life', list the ingredients and nutritional information for the label.

Planners sort out where to buy ingredients such as wheat or maize, plan how the food can be made and work out costs.

The **managing director** tells the team about the need – to design a new breakfast cereal.

Food technologists investigate how to make the breakfast cereal.

Market researchers ask the public for their ideas by using **surveys** or **questionnaires**. Later they may ask them to taste the new breakfast cereals.

Designers think about the packet design and sort out the advertising.

Finally, **reports** are written and the team talks about their work with the **managing director**.

The new breakfast cereal is ready for sale.

Later, more **reports** are written about what **changes** might be needed.

Stages in design and technology

- The **task** – to design a new breakfast cereal.
- **Ideas** – ask food technologists, market researchers, scientists.
- **Design and make** the recipe – ask a tasting panel for their views.
- Does the recipe or packing need **changing**?
- **Outcome** – a new breakfast cereal is for sale.

To do

Work in a group of about six people.

Get each member of the group to choose one of these team jobs: managing director, market researcher, food technologist, planner, scientist, designer.

Imagine that you were part of the team designing a new range of **pizzas**. Due to cutbacks the managing director has decided one of the team must go.

As a group explain how important your work is in the design of the new range of pizzas. You can act out or write and explain your job. The group must then vote to decide who is to lose their job!

Whose job goes?

Try designing a new food for yourself. You might like to invent a range of three sandwiches which could be sold in the school tuck shop at break or lunchtime. Follow the same steps as a large food maker.

What is the task?

- design three types of sandwich which could be sold in the school tuck shop.

How can you get ideas?

- Do some **research**.
1 Conduct a survey by designing a questionnaire to find out what sandwiches the students in your school would like to buy.

Here is an example of one group's questionnaire.

1 What bread do you like best?
    white ☐   brown ☐
    wholemeal ☐ other ☐

2 Do you like:
    butter ☐
    low fat spread ☐
    margarine ☐

3 What are your favourite sandwich fillings?

4 Give a new idea for a sandwich which you would buy.

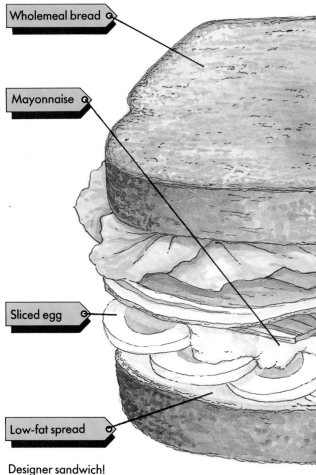

Wholemeal bread

Mayonnaise

Sliced egg

Low-fat spread

Designer sandwich!

2 Visit local bakeries, sandwich shops or large supermarkets and write down the choices of sandwiches they sell. You could ask them which was the most popular. Look at the ways sandwiches are packed and how much they cost.

Now make a *plan*.
Talk about the results of the survey and the range of sandwiches sold in shops. This should help you to decide what sandwiches you could make.

3 Design 5-10 sandwiches which you could test out.
    Think about:
- What sort of bread will you use?
- Will you use butter/margarine/low fat spread?
- What fillings will you choose?

You could draw a picture or write about your idea.

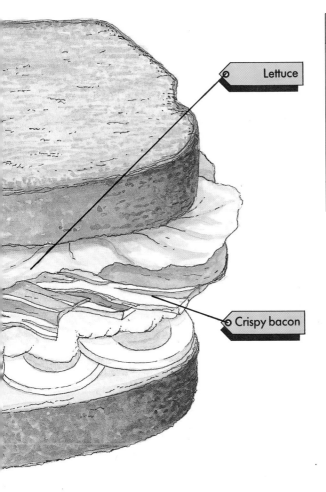

Lettuce

Crispy bacon

Cost of sandwich

Egg, bacon and lettuce sandwich.	
2 slices of bread 1 egg 1 rasher bacon	
lettuce mayonnaise low fat spread wrapping	1p 1p 1p
Total cost	

Food makers need to make a **profit** on the foods they sell. This pays for wages and the costs of the workplace.

Think about whether you want to make a profit for your school tuck shop. Write down your reasons.

8   Do you need to **advertise** your sandwiches?
    How could this be done?

9   If possible, **test out** your new sandwiches on some real customers – other students.

10 Write a short **report** on your sandwich project. You can do this even if you didn't really sell the sandwiches.
    - How successful were your ideas?
    - What problems did you meet as you worked and how did you sort them out?
    - Did anything limit what you could do – such as too little time or money?
    - What changes did you make as you worked?
    - If you had to do this task again, how could you improve the way you worked?

4   How can you **test out** your plan?
    One way is to make the sandwiches then choose the three most popular sandwiches to sell in the tuck shop.

5   How can you choose which sandwiches to sell?
    Food makers ask **tasting panels** to try out new foods for them and write a report about which they like best. Your class or group could form a tasting panel then decide which sandwiches to sell in the tuck shop.

6   Now you need to think about how to wrap up your sandwiches.
    What materials will you use?
    What about a label to describe the contents?

7   How much will you sell your sandwiches for?
    You need to work out the cost of all the ingredients. Add on a little extra to allow for waste (crusts of bread that you don't use).

Stages in design and technology

- The **task** – to design three sandwiches to sell in the tuck shop.
- **Ideas** – make a survey, visit local shops.
- Plan and **test out** ideas – form a tasting panel.
- **Report** on what you have done and make **changes**.

Since the 1960s in Britain and America people are eating more and more fast, takeaway food.

What is the reason for these changes in our eating habits?

- More women go out to work and may not be home at meal times.
- We have more money to spend.
- Technology has improved the ways of making fast foods.
- People seem to like it!

Question

Why do you think we are eating more fast, takeaway food? Add two ideas of your own.

Fast food shop

Big Macs

Fast food means technology

Let's look at the history of McDonald's. In the time it takes to read this sentence, 300 McDonald's burgers will be cooked – that's 12 million a day! In 1954 an American, Ray Kroc, copied the idea of a Californian hamburger and milkshake stand run by Dick and Maurice McDonald. Mr Kroc decided that his burgers should have an exact recipe, grill heat, cooking time and amounts of ketchup and mustard. That way his customers always knew what they were buying.

Stages in design and technology

- The **task** – to design a fast hamburger restaurant.
- **Ideas** – copy the McDonald's milkshake stall.
- **Outcome** – over 10,000 McDonald's restaurants worldwide!
- **Improvements** – test out new ideas all the time.

Fast food is not fast to invent. It takes years of research, new developments in technology and thorough testing before a new food is ready.

To do

1 Imagine that you were opening a fast food shop which served takeaway meals made from eggs.

Scrambled eggs

You can cook them on the hob or in the microwave.

Ingredients
two eggs, size 3
little milk
salt and pepper
10 g margarine

Equipment
bowl
fork
saucepan
wooden spoon

Method
1 Beat together the eggs, milk, salt and pepper.
2 **Either** melt the margarine in a saucepan, pour in the eggs and cook over a gentle heat until thick,
Or put all the ingredients in a bowl and place in the microwave. Cook on full power for 1 minute. Stir then cook again until firm.

---

2 Now **design a range of fillings** which you can mix with scrambled eggs to serve in a bun.

Here are some ideas. You may have others.

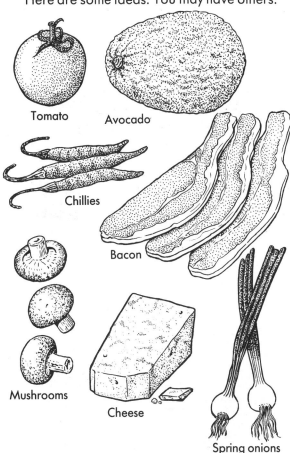

Tomato   Avocado

Chillies

Bacon

Mushrooms

Cheese

Spring onions

3 Test out one idea using the scrambled egg recipe.
4 **Design a menu** to show the choice you could offer.
5 How could you **improve** on the work you have done?
6 The diagram shows the design for a 'perfect burger'. Draw your own 'scrambled egg bun' and decide how you will fill it.

Sesame seeds — really crunchy

Bun top

Relish

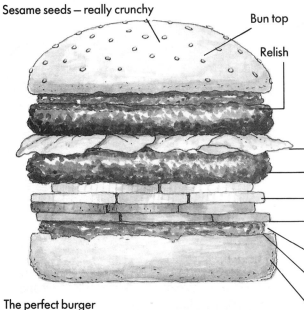

Lettuce — must be crisp

100% beef patties — really beefy

Onion slices — got to be sweet

Tomato slices — just ripe

Pickle slices — got to be tangy

Relish — got to be tasty

Bun bottom

The perfect burger

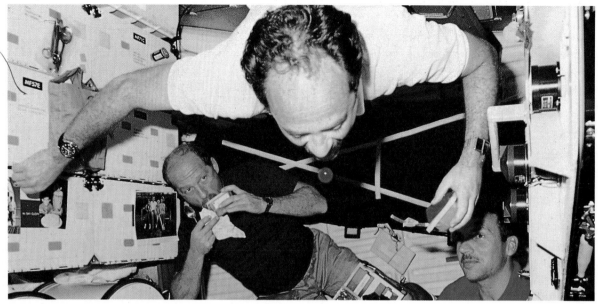

Living room in a space craft (strawberry drink floats in a round ball)

Imagine that you had to supply the food for a space trip to the moon for the astronauts in the Space Shuttle. Think about the problems!

- You must include all the food that they need for the trip – there are no shops in space!
- You need food to keep fresh and ready to eat for the whole voyage.
- Astronauts are floating around as they cook and eat your food, because in space everything is weightless.
- Meals must be easy to prepare – they have no time to peel potatoes and cannot just throw the rubbish out of the spacecraft!
- Food must be packed to save weight and packing space – the computers and space equipment take up most of the room in the spacecraft.
- Astronauts like a choice of drinks and ready to eat meals – otherwise they get bored.

Did you know?

On the first space missions, **food technologists** thought that soup might explode out of the soup bowls, and sandwiches and cutlery would float away in the weightlessness of space. So, the first astronauts sucked from squeezy tubes and ate food made into chewy tablets. **Yuk!**

So how have food technologists solved the space food problem?

- Most food on the latest Space Shuttles is dried into a powder – you just add water, mix and heat it up.
- Meat and fruit is preserved and packed into cans or foil pouches.
- Nuts, biscuits and chocolate bars are packed the same as on earth.

Space meal

Space meal notes for astronauts

On your space trip you can have **three main meals a day**, providing a total of 12 540 kJ.

Water is made by the spacecraft's fuel system, so you don't need to carry any on board.

You can choose from **75 types of food** and **20 drinks** – the menu comes round **every six days**.

Each astronaut must **take their turn** at cooking, serving and clearing up.

Wash your hands in the plastic dome washbasin – the water is drawn up by air flow and won't splash all over the cabin.

Meals take about 20 minutes to prepare – just add water to the packets of dried food, shake and mix, then heat it in the electric oven.

Drinks like coffee or orange are freeze dried – just add hot or cold water.

Suck drinks through a straw and clip the straw after each suck, otherwise the drink will float out into the cabin in a round ball!

Washing up – put empty food containers in the shuttle's dustbin under the floor of the mid deck.

Clean trays and utensils with wet wipes. Mop up spills with paper towels or the small vacuum cleaner.

Questions

1 Imagine that you were the food technologist responsible for the next space mission. Plan a day's meals for four astronauts. Decide how the food will be packed and how it can be prepared. Copy the chart below and fill in your ideas. One drink has already been completed.

Meals for one day on the space mission	How they are packed	How they are prepared
breakfast: orange juice	dried and packed in foil pouch	add cold water, mix and drink with a straw

2 Look at the label for the Space Bar. How has the ice cream been prepared and packed for the space mission? Why do you think this food has been chosen for the trip?

3 What new problems will food technologists have to face when planning meals for longer space journeys? Make a list of foods or even animals and plants which might be taken on board the space craft.

The Space Bar

People who are blind, in wheelchairs or old and frail may find cooking a difficult business.

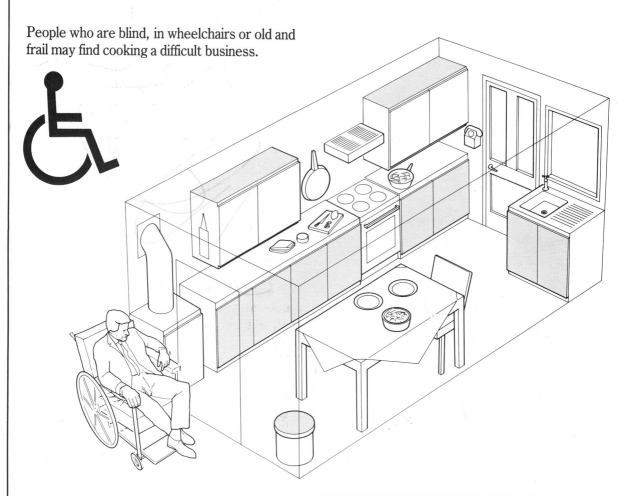

Problems for disabled people

Designing a meal for a disabled person D

What is it like to prepare a meal if you are disabled? Work in small groups. Plan and prepare a simple snack meal for yourselves such as poached egg on toast with a pot of tea.

Choose one group member to act out the role of a disabled person, perhaps blind or frail. As you work, write down any problems the disabled person might have in cooking this meal. What might make the work easier?

Write down the changes you would make to a kitchen to make it safer for a disabled person to use.

Stages in design and technology

- The **task** – to design a kitchen for disabled people who are perhaps blind or frail.
- **Ideas** – think about what it is like to be disabled – test out a meal.

To do

1 Look at the kitchen in the picture. Imagine that you were disabled and had to use a wheelchair. List *five* things in this kitchen which might be dangerous or difficult for you to use.

2 How could you adapt (change) this kitchen to make your work easier?

Technology has helped to make many jobs around the home easier and safer. Automatic electric kettles which switch off when the water boils are safer for blind people who might be scalded if they cannot see a kettle boiling.

Gas ovens with automatic ignition save an elderly person struggling with matches.

Here are some gadgets and equipment specially designed to help disabled people in the kitchen.

Help for the disabled around the kitchen

Nelson knife: designed for Admiral Nelson so that he could cut up then eat food using only one hand. £6.75

Teapot pourer stand: to make pouring safer and easier, since the teapot will not fall off. £8.99

Easiturn tap turner: a strong plastic lever which fits over taps to make them easy to turn. Braille symbols for the blind tell them whether the tap is hot or cold. £2.95

Lid lifter: a handle to lift off hot saucepan lids. £2.25

(All details from *Boots Healthcare in the Home* – Boots the Chemists Ltd, Nottingham NG2 3AA)

Questions

1 Choose *two* of these gadgets and show how they could help a blind person prepare a meal.
2 Which *two* pieces of equipment do you think are the most useful for disabled people? Give your reasons.
3 Design a new kitchen gadget which could help a disabled person prepare a meal for themselves. Draw and label your design and explain why it is useful.

Further work

Visit your local shops and make a list of *five* pieces of equipment, or special gadgets which can help with meal preparation if you have some handicap. Your local Gas or Electricity showroom should give you ideas. To find out more information, you could write to:
● Disabled Living Foundation, 380–384 Harrow Road, London W9 2HU,
● Help the Aged, St James Walk, London EC1R 0BE,
● Royal National Institute for the Blind, 224 Great Portland St, London W1.

When it comes to feeding young children, there are some special needs to think about.

- They have just learnt to sit and maybe stand on their own, so they need special chairs and tables if they are to be safe.

- Their feeding equipment must be carefully designed so that they can try to feed themselves without getting hurt.

- Equipment must be easy to clean. Germs can make young children very sick.

- If they have just started to eat other foods as well as milk, their food must be mashed up and stored in clean containers.

Stages in design and technology

- **The need** – to design a dish to help feed a baby or toddler.
- **Ideas** – ask a scientist to invent an unbreakable material.
- **Outcome** – a range of special, unbreakable, easy to clean plastic dishes.
- **Improvements** – now design better shapes and sizes.

To do

1 Look at the five gadgets on page 19 for feeding young children.
2 Choose two gadgets which you think would most help a baby feed itself. Explain why you made these choices.
3 What special points have to be thought about when designing gadgets for feeding young children?
4 Design a piece of equipment for feeding babies or toddlers. Draw and label your design and explain what special points you have thought about which will help the baby to feed itself.

All these feeding items are nearly unbreakable and easy to wash and sterilize.

1 Non-slip cereal bowl with egg-cup top: the top section can be removed so you can use the bowl for cereals. A suction pad holds the bowl firmly on the table. £2.99 (Mothercare)

2 Weaning spoon, spoon and fork set: weaning spoon is narrow for easy feeding; extra long handles help child feed itself. £0.90 (Mothercare)

3 Beaker and cup: light and easy to hold, with spout to stop drinks spilling; marked for accurate measuring. £1.65 (Mothercare)

4 Non-slip cereal bowl: with high sides to help child feed itself; rubber suction pad stops slipping. £2.25 (Mothercare)

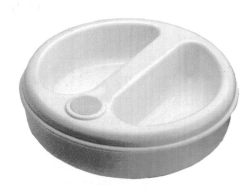

5 Stay-warm plate: two compartments and suction pad; hot water in base helps keep food warm, but child cannot put fingers into it. £2.99 (Mothercare)

Babies have special needs when it comes to food. Here are some of the **constraints** – the special things to think about – when feeding babies.

Look at the label for apricot custard. Think about whether it meets the constraints shown when feeding babies.

I don't need salt or sugar added to my food.

Can I have natural food please?

I only have a few teeth, so I don't like tough, chewy food.

Don't make my food too hot or cold.

HEINZ
FROM 3 to 9 MONTHS

e 128 g

APRICOT CUSTARD

CONTAINS NON-MILK FAT

✓ NO ADDED SALT
✓ NO ADDED PRESERVATIVES
✓ NO ARTIFICIAL COLOURS
✓ NO ARTIFICIAL FLAVOURS
✓ GLUTEN FREE

PER CAN PER 100 g	FAT	PROTEIN	CARBOHYDRATE	ENERGY
	1.2 g 0.9 g	17 g 13 g	17.0 g 13.3 g	345 kJ (81 kcal) 268 kJ (63 kcal)

MADE IN ENGLAND
H J HEINZ CO LTD
HAYES MIDDX UB4 8AL

Heinz Baby Foods have been carefully prepared using only pure ingredients and will help provide a nutritionally balanced diet. Do not add sugar or salt. PREPARATION: Serve cold or warm. To heat, stand a covered cup containing required amount in hot water. The unwarmed portion should be covered and will safely store in a refrigerator for up to 48 hours. For the Heinz Baby Club brochure (UK only) free feeding guide and advice write to Susan Baxter at the address above.

INGREDIENTS: WATER, SKIMMED MILK APRICOTS, PINEAPPLE JUICE, SUGAR MODIFIED CORNFLOUR, EGGS, LEMON JUICE RICE, TAPIOCA, VEGETABLE OIL VITAMIN C (minimum 15mg/100g)

Apricot custard

Questions

Use the label to answer the questions.
1 Why is this food suitable for babies?
2 Are natural ingredients used? How do you know?
3 Use other books to find out why some baby food is 'gluten free'.

To do D

Design a new baby food.
- Get some **ideas** – look around the shops, and ask the families what their babies like to eat. (Books and leaflets from health clinics can help too.)
- **Plan** the food you are going to make. Does it meet the **constraints** shown above?
- **Test out** your recipe – try it on a real baby!
- Do you need to make any **changes** to the recipe?

Use a computer!

If you were in the food business, you would need to **advertise** your new food in order to sell it.

How would you design an advertisement?

Collect advertisements from magazines and newspapers to give you ideas. Talk with other members of your group and think about why some advertisements are more successful than others.

Now **design** your own advertisement. It could be a poster, a radio jingle, a computer designed printout for a newspaper or even a video!

Old advertising

Design an advert

Questions

Ideas on what babies should eat have changed over the years. Today experts believe that children should eat a variety of foods. That way they get a range of nutrients which is important for good health.

Look at this old advertisement for Ridge's Food.

1 What claims are made about what this baby food can do?
2 Today advertisements must tell the truth. Do you think all the claims made in this old advertisement are true?
3 Why do you think children should be given a variety of foods and not just one?

Technology is about changing the things around us to suit our needs. In the 1980s several Government reports recommended that in Britain we should change the sorts of food that we eat. Here are their simple rules for healthy eating:

- eat more fibre-rich foods – especially from cereal foods,
- eat fewer fatty foods, especially those containing animal fats,
- eat less sugar,
- eat less salt.

So, the food makers had to change the range of food for sale to meet the **needs** of the customer – you! They had to try and make their food more healthy.

To do

Work in small groups. Look at the collection of food labels. Each label makes claims about how healthy the food is to eat. Make your own collection of 'healthy eating' food labels like the ones shown here.

Discuss which foods make claims about:
(a) fibre content,
(b) lower fat,
(c) the amount of sugar,
(d) low salt.

Now think about how the food makers might have changed that food to fit in with our ideas on healthy eating.

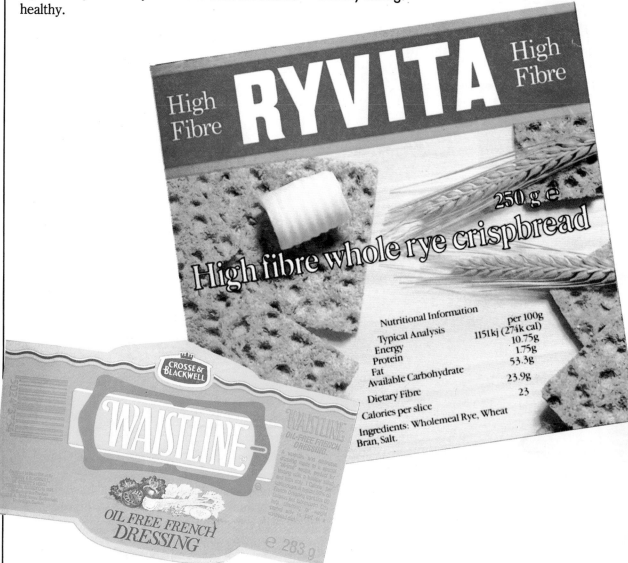

High Fibre **RYVITA** High Fibre

High Fibre

250 g ℮

High fibre whole rye crispbread

Nutritional Information	
Typical Analysis	per 100g
Energy	1151kj (274k cal)
Protein	10.75g
Fat	1.75g
Available Carbohydrate	53.3g
Dietary Fibre	23.9g
Calories per slice	23

Ingredients: Wholemeal Rye, Wheat Bran, Salt.

CROSSE & BLACKWELL

WAISTLINE

OIL FREE FRENCH DRESSING

℮ 283 g

Skimmed milk with non-milk fat

kerrygold

LOW FAT MAX. 1.8% FAT

Light

Skimmed milk with non-milk fat

All the taste of milk – less than half the fat

Fill in for yourself the 'Stages in design and technology' for the need below.

Stages in design and technology

- The **need** – customers want a healthier can of baked beans
- **Ideas**
- **Outcome**

SAINSBURY'S

BEANS

in tomato sauce

447 gram 15¾ oz

REDUCED SUGAR, REDUCED SALT

HIGH FIBRE

SAINSBURY'S UNSWEETENED PEACH SLICES

WITH PEACH JUICE

IN FRUIT JUICE

LOW CALORIE
NO ADDED SUGAR

LO SALT

REDUCED SODIUM SALT ALTERNATIVE

USE AS ORDINARY COOKING AND TABLE SALT

Since we should try to eat less fat, salt and sugar and more dietary fibre, old recipes must be changed to fit in with our healthier way of life.

Here is a traditional recipe for Spaghetti Bolognese. The cook has written in the changes to be made to make the recipe healthier.

Serves 2   **Spaghetti Bolognese**

Ingredients

25g butter   *leave out*
4 tablespoons oil   *leave out*
1 small onion finely chopped
225 g minced beef — *use 'extra lean'*
15 g plain flour — *use wholemeal flour*
1 small can tomatoes (about 200 g)
salt and pepper, mixed herbs — *only a very little*
100 g spaghetti — *use wholewheat spaghetti*

Equipment

2 saucepans   chopping board
lid   tablespoon
wooden spoon
knife

Method

leave out

1 Heat the butter and oil in a pan and fry the onions and the meat until the meat browns.
2 Stir in the flour then add the tomatoes, salt and pepper and herbs.
3 Boil, then lower the heat, and cover and simmer for 15 minutes.
4 Cook the spaghetti according to packet instructions.
5 Serve the sauce poured over the hot spaghetti.

To do

1 Make a list of the ingredients in the recipe which have been changed. In each case, explain why you think the changes have been made.
2 Find a recipe from an old cookery book which you would like to make. Try and change that recipe to fit in with modern ideas on healthy eating.
3 Write out the healthier recipe, then test it out. You could compare the old and the new recipe to see which you prefer.

Questions

1 If you were a food maker, how would you try to change the following types of food to suit the needs of your customers?
(a) lower the amount of salt in Shepherd's Pie,
(b) cut down on the amount of fat in a range of biscuits,
(c) add more fibre to your white bread,
(d) cut down the amount of sugar in your orange drink?

Healthy Spaghetti Bolognese

Using computers to help

Computer programs such as The Food Program (ILECC) contain vast amounts of information about the food value of foods. Computers are quick to use and can print out information in the form of bar charts and pie charts to help compare results. We used the computer to compare the food values of (a) Spaghetti Bolognese (p. 24) and a healthier recipe, (b) traditional apple crumble (p. 27) and a higher fibre recipe. Here are the results, printed out as bar charts.

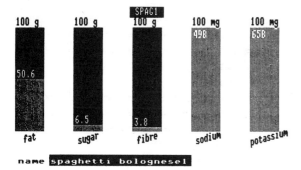

SPAG1

100 g	100 g	100 g	100 mg	100 mg
			498	658
50.6				
	6.5	3.8		
fat	sugar	fibre	sodium	potassium

name **spaghetti bolognese1**

Lunch

140	BUTTER, SALTED	10.00 g	
198	MAIZE (CORN) OIL	30.00 g	
613	ONIONS, RAW	35.00 g	
1075	MINCED BEEF, AVERAGE	110.00 g	
14	FLOUR WHITE PATENT (40%)	12.00 g	
668	TOMATOES, CANNED	100.00 g	
26	SPAGHETTI, RAW	50.00 g	

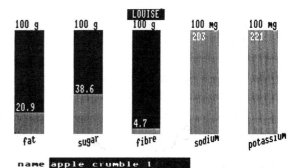

LOUISE

100 g	100 g	100 g	100 mg	100 mg
			203	231
	38.6			
20.9				
		4.7		
fat	sugar	fibre	sodium	potassium

name **apple crumble 1**

Lunch

677	APPLES COOKING, RAW	125.00 g	
843	SUGAR WHITE	25.00 g	
12	FLOUR, WHITE HOUSEHOLD, PLAIN	50.00 g	
187	margarine-all kinds	25.00 g	

LEAN

100 g	100 g	100 g	100 mg	100 mg
			556	695
11.5	4.2	7.7		
fat	sugar	fibre	sodium	potassium

name **spaghetti bolognese2**

Lunch

613	ONIONS, RAW	35.00 g	
1069	MINCED BEEF, LEAN, STEWED	110.00 g	
9	FLOUR WHOLEMEAL (100%)	12.00 g	
668	TOMATOES, CANNED	100.00 g	
1005	PASTA, WHOLEMEAL, RAW	50.00 g	

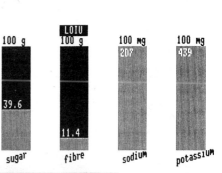

LOIU

100 g	100 g	100 g	100 mg	100 mg
			207	439
	39.6			
27.8				
		11.4		
fat	sugar	fibre	sodium	potassium

name **apple crumble 2**

677	APPLES COOKING, RAW	125.00 g	
843	SUGAR WHITE	25.00 g	
9	FLOUR WHOLEMEAL (100%)	50.00 g	
187	margarine-all kinds	25.00 g	
54	SHREDDED WHEAT	10.00 g	
834	COCONUT, DESICCATED	10.00 g	

To do

1 Use the bar charts for Spaghetti Bolognese. The healthier recipe (Spaghetti Bolognese 2) contains less fat and more fibre. How do the bar charts show these results?
2 Use the bar charts for apple crumble 1 and 2 (higher fibre recipe). How do the bar charts show that recipe 2 contains more fibre?

What foods have been added to the recipe to provide this extra fibre?

Try using computer programs for yourself. They can compare food values, and also help you plan a healthy diet for yourself.

Food fashions in fibre

In the past, it was poor people who ate high fibre foods such as wholemeal bread and plenty of root vegetables. Technology changed all that – white flour became cheaper so people ate lower fibre white bread. But then in the 1980s health reports suggested that we should eat more dietary fibre.

So we need to eat more fruits and vegetables, peas and beans, and especially **cereals** with their high-fibre **bran** coating.

Now food technologists are inventing new ways to increase the amount of dietary fibre in the foods we eat.

To do

1 Look at the *two* bread labels. What ingredients provide dietary fibre? How much dietary fibre is in 100 g of each bread?
2 Collect some bread labels of your own. You could use a computer to draw up a bar or pie chart to compare the amount of dietary fibre in the different breads. Look up any of the words on the labels that you don't understand.
3 Visit your local shops and make a list of the different kinds of food which claim to be 'high fibre'. Compare your list with the rest of the class.
4 Breads of the future! Imagine that you had to design a bread for the year 2001. Describe what it would contain and look like. How would it fit in with the new century? What might the customers demand then?
5 Fill in the 'Stages in design and technology' below for the need 'people want healthier, high fibre food'.

WINDMILL — THE WINDMILL BAKERY

WHITE BREAD WITH ADDED VEGETABLE FIBRE

INGREDIENTS

Unbleached, untreated flour, water, pea bran (6.4%), yeast, dried glucose syrup, salt, wheat protein, hydrogenated vegetable oil, vinegar, emulsifiers: E471, E472(e) (improves the eating qualities of the bread), soya flour, flour improvers: ascorbic acid (vitamin C), 924.

NUTRITIONAL INFORMATION

Typical Analysis	Per 100g
Energy	950kJ (225kcal)
Protein	6.7g
Carbohydrate	48.0g
Fat	1.9g
Salt	1.0g
Dietary Fibre	8.6g

SAINSBURY'S 6 STONEGROUND WHOLEMEAL BAPS

SUITABLE FOR HOME FREEZING

INGREDIENTS: WHOLEMEAL FLOUR, WATER, WHEAT PROTEIN, YEAST, DRIED GLUCOSE SYRUP, HYDROGENATED VEGETABLE OIL, SALT, VINEGAR, EMULSIFIERS: E471, E472(e); SOYA FLOUR, FLOUR IMPROVER: L-ASCORBIC ACID.

HIGH FIBRE
NO ARTIFICIAL PRESERVATIVES

Best within 1 day of purchase

NUTRITION	TYPICAL VALUES PER 100g (3½ oz)	TYPICAL VALUES PER BAP
ENERGY	225 k.CALORIES	125 k.CAL
	960 k.JOULES	525 k.JO
PROTEIN	11.0 g	6.1 g
CARBOHYDRATE AVAILABLE	37.6 g	20.7
TOTAL FAT	4.1 g	2.3
DIETARY FIBRE	8.3 g	4.6
ADDED SUGARS	1.3 g	0.
ADDED SALT	1.3 g	0.

Produced for J Sainsbury plc Stamford Stre

Two bread labels

Stages in design and technology

- The **need** – people want healthier, high fibre food.
- **ideas**
- **Outcome**

Traditional apple crumble

Ingredients
250 g /1 large cooking apple, peeled and sliced
1 tablespoon sugar
topping: 100 g plain white flour
50 g soft margarine
25 g caster sugar

Equipment
knife
chopping board
ovenproof dish
mixing bowl
tablespoon

Method
1 Set the oven at 190°C/Gas mark 5.
2 Place the fruit in an ovenproof dish and sprinkle over the sugar.
3 Put the flour in a bowl and rub in the margarine with your fingertips until the mixture resembles breadcrumbs. Toss in the sugar.
4 Sprinkle the crumble over the fruit and bake in the oven for 30 minutes until the fruit is soft and the crumble a pale golden colour.
5 Serve hot or cold with custard, ice cream or yoghurt.

To do D

The amount of dietary fibre in the recipe could be increased by adding fibre-rich ingredients or replacing the white flour with wholemeal flour.

1 Invent a higher fibre apple crumble recipe of your own.

Tips

- Add extra ingredients from the list below.
- Swop the white flour for higher fibre foods.
- Unpeeled apples contain more fibre.

List to show dietary fibre in 100 grams of foods

Foods	Amount of dietary fibre in 100 grams
white flour	3g
wholemeal flour	9g
oatmeal	8g
wheat bran	36g
Shredded Wheat	10g
All Bran	25g
desiccated coconut	14g

Englyst method of analysis of dietary fibre

Now write out the ingredients for your higher fibre apple crumble recipe. Measure, weigh and write down exactly the amounts that you choose.

2 **Test out** your recipe to see if it works.

3 Compare the different recipes for apple crumble which your group has invented. **Look** at them and **taste** them, then decide which recipe you like best. Write a sentence to explain why you made this choice.

4 You could try and work out the amount of dietary fibre in the recipe.

The ingredients

Four hundred years ago, sugar was a new food in Britain. Today we each eat 37 kilograms a year! Now health experts suggest we eat less sugar since too much sugar can cause tooth decay.

The history of sugar

Sugar cane was brought to Britain in the 16th century. Before that, people sweetened their food with honey and dried fruit. Soon sugar cane was grown in many hot parts of the world, and exported to other countries.

One raisin or two ?

Stages in design and technology

- The **need** – wars in Europe cut off sugar cane supplies.
- **Ideas** – French scientists tried to get sugar from sweet root vegetables.
- **Outcome** – 1801 – the world's first sugar beet factory.
- **Improvements** – sugar beet factories open all over Europe.

Artificial sweeteners

Today, some people want to eat sweet foods without eating sugar. So scientists have invented artificial sweeteners which make food sweet but provide less energy than sugar (fewer kilojoules/kilocalories). These are used in drinks and foods.

To do

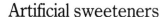

Compare sugar with artificial sweeteners.
Work in groups.

You need:
600 ml/1 pint unsweetened custard made up to packet instructions
some sugar
2-3 different artificial sweeteners
3-4 bowls
teaspoons

Method:
1 Read the instructions for each sweetener to find out how much is needed to sweeten as much as two teaspoons of sugar.
2 Divide the custard between 3 – 4 bowls, depending on how many sweeteners you use.
3 Sweeten each bowl of custard with two teaspoons of sugar or the same sweetness (equivalent) of artificial sweetener.
4 Now use a teaspoon and taste each bowl of custard.
Draw up a chart like the one below and fill in your details.

Sweetener	How sweet is it?	Comments
Sugar	5/10	

Which sweetener did you prefer and why?

Sugar free drinks

Low calorie soft drinks are sugar free and useful for people who are watching their weight and don't want to eat too much sugar. **Saccharin** was discovered 100 years ago and is 550 times as sweet as sugar. **Aspartame** is another non-sugar sweetener, discovered in 1965 and used to sweeten drinks.

To do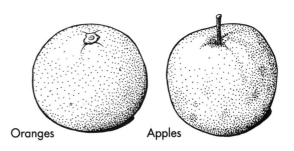

Make a collection of cans and labels from soft drinks which claim to be 'low calorie' or 'sugar free'.

Look at the soft drink label. What sweetener has been used? What claims are made about how this drink is sweetened? You could count up the number of times different sweeteners are used for drinks, then draw up a chart to show your results.

How else can you sweeten food?

Fruits, especially raisins, sultanas, dates and dried apricots are very sweet. Try eating apples and oranges instead of sugary sweets.

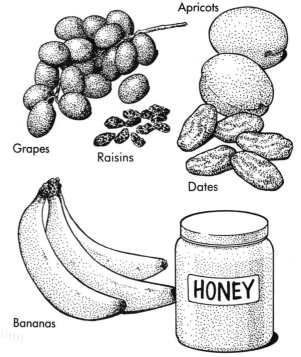

Oranges   Apples

Apricots

Grapes

Raisins

Dates

Bananas

HONEY

SHAPERS
Best Before End

Boots

Tropical Fruit
Low Calorie Drink

Made with a blend of 10 fruit juices.
CONTAINS 25% FRUIT JUICE. NO ADDED SUGAR.
FREE FROM ARTIFICIAL COLOURS AND FLAVOURS. SEE FOOD FACTS.

SWEETENED WITH
NUTRASWEET BLEND
BRAND SWEETENER

50 ml

Fat   0.2 gram
Carbohydrate   Negligible
Energy Value   2.7 gram
                              65 kJ
                              15 kcal (Calories)

Shake well before use. Dilute to taste.
Store in a cool place.
Boots Brand Foods contain only natural
or nature identical colours and flavours.

* NutraSweet is a registered trademark of The NutraSweet Company
INGREDIENTS: Water, Fruit Juices (Orange, Apple, Pineapple, Passion
Fruit, Guava, Apricot, Mandarin, Mango, Banana, Lime), Citric Acid, Acidity
Regulator (Sodium Citrate), Stabiliser (E466), Flavouring, Artificial
Sweeteners (†Aspartame, Sodium Saccharin), Preservatives (Sodium
Metabisulphite, Sodium Benzoate).
† Contains Phenylalanine
This product can help slimming or weight control only as part of a
Calorie-controlled diet.
THE BOOTS COMPANY PLC NOTTINGHAM ENGLAND

Shapers label

Further work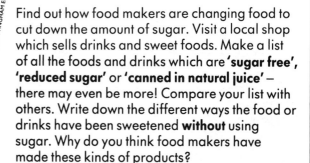

Find out how food makers are changing food to cut down the amount of sugar. Visit a local shop which sells drinks and sweet foods. Make a list of all the foods and drinks which are **'sugar free'**, **'reduced sugar'** or **'canned in natural juice'** – there may even be more! Compare your list with others. Write down the different ways the food or drinks have been sweetened **without** using sugar. Why do you think food makers have made these kinds of products?

Changing the fats we eat

Health experts think that we should eat **less fat**, so food makers are creating fat spreads with **lower fat content**. Experts also believe that eating too many **saturated fatty acids**, which are mainly found in animal fat such as butter, can lead to heart disease. They suggest that we eat more **polyunsaturated fatty acids**, like those in some vegetable oils.

Now draw up two bar charts to compare:
(a) the total fat content in the fat spreads,
(b) the amounts of saturated and polyunsaturated fatty acids.
You could use a **computer** to help.

Stages in design and technology

- The **need** – people want healthier, lower fat spreads.
- **Ideas** – ask food technologists and scientists for ideas.
- **Outcome** – many more vegetable oil and lower fat spreads are sold.
- That's technology! Changing the food we eat to suit our needs.

To do

What is in the fat spreads we eat?
Make a collection of labels of different margarines and fat spreads. Use information from your labels and the three labels on page 31 to fill in the chart below.

Fat chart

		Nutrients in 100 grams	
Name of fat spread	Total fats	Saturated fatty acids	Polyunsaturated fatty acids
soft margarine	80 g	19.2 g	40.8 g
butter			
Taflo			

How can you work out the amount of water and other ingredients? Well, 100g margarine contains 80g fat, so 20g must be water and...

Bar chart to show the amount of fat in 100g of spreads

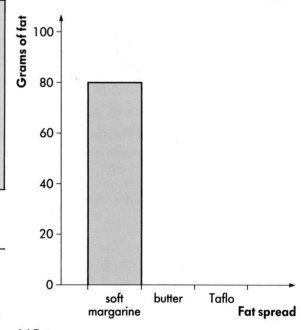

(a) Fats

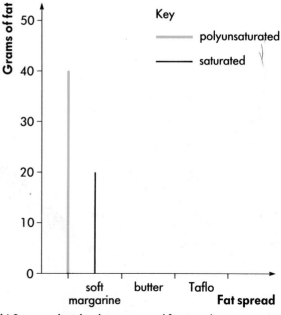

(b) Saturated and polyunsaturated fatty acids

TAFLÖ
low fat sunflower spread

HIGH IN TASTE. HIGH IN POLYUNSATURATES

LOW IN SATURATES. LOW IN CHOLESTEROL

keep refrigerated 500g

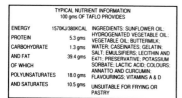

TYPICAL NUTRIENT INFORMATION
100 gms OF TAFLO PROVIDES

ENERGY	1570KJ/380KCAL	INGREDIENTS: SUNFLOWER OIL: HYDROGENATED VEGETABLE OIL: VEGETABLE OIL: BUTTERMILK: WATER: CASEINATES: GELATIN: SALT: EMULSIFIERS: LECITHIN AND E471: PRESERVATIVE: POTASSIUM SORBATE: LACTIC ACID: COLOURS: ANNATTO AND CURCUMIN: FLAVOURINGS: VITAMINS A & D
PROTEIN	5.3 gms	
CARBOHYDRATE	1.3 gms	
AND FAT	39.4 gms	
OF WHICH		
POLYUNSATURATES	18.0 gms	
AND SATURATES	10.5 gms	UNSUITABLE FOR FRYING OR PASTRY

KEEP REFRIGERATED
ADDED INGREDIENTS: SALT

DAIRY BUTTER 250g

DAIRY BUTTER

English Butter   250g

Nutritional Analysis

	per 100g
Protein	0.4g
Total Fat	82g
of which Polyunsaturated Fatty Acids	2.2g
Saturated Fatty Acids	49g
Energy value	3041 kJ
	740 kcal
	(Calories)

What's in a spread?

1 Which fat spread contains:
   (a) the most fat,
   (b) the least fat?

2 Which fat is highest in:
   (a) saturated fatty acids,
   (b) polyunsaturated fatty acids?

3 Which spread would you suggest for someone who:
   (a) wanted to eat healthily,
   (b) had a heart condition,
   (c) wanted to lose weight?
   Give your reasons.

IDEAL FOR SPREADING

AND COOKING

Spreado
Soft Margarine

NUTRITIONAL GUIDE
TYPICAL CONTENTS PER 100 g
TOTAL FAT 80 g OF WHICH 51%
(40.8 g) IS POLYUNSATURATED AND
24% (19.2 g) IS SATURATED
ENERGY 740 K CALORIES
CHOLESTEROL 0.001 g

Further work

People are trying to eat less fat. Food makers have had to change the sorts of food they sell to meet this 'customer demand'. Find out how different foods are changing to meet this need. For example, you can buy skimmed, lower fat milk instead of whole milk.

Interview people, using a tape recorder, and ask them how they try to eat less fat. You could make a display to show the rest of the school how to cut down on the fat they eat.

Look at recipes. How can you change them to use less fat? Why not print a **healthy low fat recipe book** using the **wordprocessor** program on your computer?

How do we make flour?

First of all, what is meant by flour? Flour can be made by grinding up different dried foods. Around the world, flours can be made from cereals, seeds and roots. Flour is easier to eat and digest than whole grains or seeds.

Here are some examples of cereals, seeds and roots made into flours.

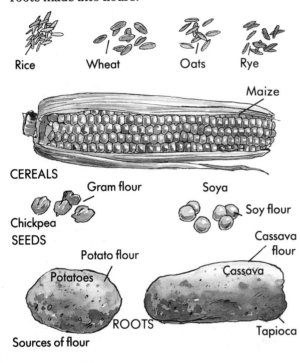

Rice   Wheat   Oats   Rye

Maize

CEREALS

Gram flour   Soya

Chickpea   Soy flour

SEEDS

Potato flour   Cassava flour

Potatoes   Cassava

ROOTS   Tapioca

Sources of flour

To do

Test out ways to grind your own flour. You could use some cereal seeds such as wheat, barley, rice or oats to make a powder. Compare results with others and suggest the best method.

Question

Find a recipe which uses each of the following foods for flour:
(a) cereals, (b) peas or beans, (c) roots.

How is technology changing the way flour is milled?

Most flour is made from wheat. Years ago wheat was ground between two stones to make flour. This process is called **milling**. In the 11th century in Britain, windmills and watermills were used to grind flour, but after the **Industrial Revolution** flour was milled by machinery. New technology means that flour can be milled in automated mills which is more efficient and lowers the cost.

Milling flour

Stages in design and technology

- The **need** – to find out how to grind things to make them easier to cook.
- **Ideas** – see how other people grind food and experiment.
- **Outcome** – different grinding and milling methods all around the world.
- **Constraints** – methods around the world depend on the type of power which can be used (electricity, water or people), how much money can be spent on equipment and the amount of food to be ground.

How is wheat made into flour?

First look at the cross-section of a wheat grain. Notice that the grain is divided into three parts:
- the outside **bran** (source of fibre),
- the floury **endosperm** (makes the flour),
- the **germ** (source of protein) where the seed sprouts.

To do

Find out how much bran there is in the different flours. Sieve 100 grams of different flours three or four times, through a fine sieve, into a bowl. Collect what is left in the sieve – this is some of the bran. Notice that the sieved flour has become paler once some of the bran has been removed. Put the bran from each flour on a plate and compare the results. Which flour contained the largest amount of bran?

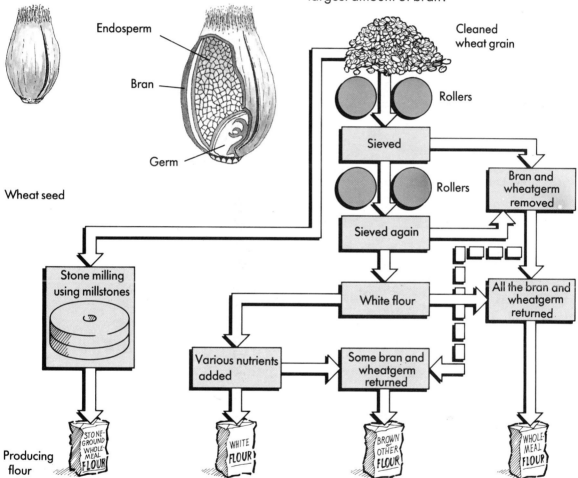

Endosperm

Bran

Germ

Wheat seed

Cleaned wheat grain

Rollers

Sieved

Rollers

Bran and wheatgerm removed

Sieved again

Stone milling using millstones

White flour

All the bran and wheatgerm returned

Various nutrients added

Some bran and wheatgerm returned

Producing flour

STONE-GROUND WHOLE-MEAL FLOUR

WHITE FLOUR

BROWN OTHER FLOUR

WHOLE-MEAL FLOUR

The chart shows how different flours are made from wheat.

Questions

1 In your own words, describe how: (a) white, (b) wholemeal, (c) stoneground flour are made.

2 Visit your local food shop and make a list of the different kinds of flour for sale. Why do you think there is such a variety?

Bread today

Bread can be made from different cereals such as rye, oats, barley and even peas and beans. With more food coming to Britain from around the world, so a wider variety of bread is made and sold in Britain.

Chart to show variety of breads on sale in Britain today

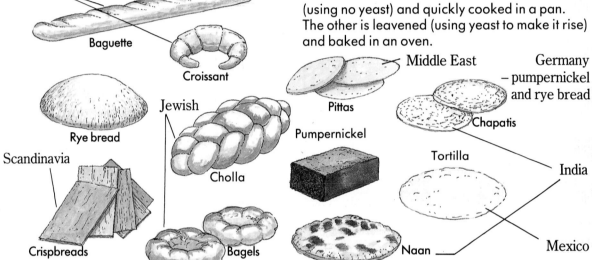

France
Baguette
Croissant
Rye bread
Scandinavia
Jewish
Cholla
Crispbreads
Bagels
Pittas
Pumpernickel
Middle East
Naan
Tortilla
Chapatis
Germany – pumpernickel and rye bread
India
Mexico

Questions

1 Name *two* breads which are not made from wheat flour.
2 Use other books to find out how to make *one* of the breads shown on the chart.

To do

Work in small groups and make *two* different sorts of bread. One is unleavened Indian bread, (using no yeast) and quickly cooked in a pan. The other is leavened (using yeast to make it rise) and baked in an oven.

Chapatis

Ingredients
200 g wholewheat or chapati flour
1 teaspoon salt
125 ml (approx) water

Equipment
bowl
jug
teaspoon
wooden spoon
frying pan
palette knife

Method
1 Place the flour and salt in a bowl and work to a stiff dough with water. Add more water if necessary.
2 Knead the dough by pressing and squeezing it with your hands on the work surface to make it smooth.
3 Cover the dough with cling film or a tea towel for 30 minutes.
4 Divide into 12 equal pieces. Sprinkle a little flour on the work surface then roll each piece of dough into a thin circle.
5 Heat a non-stick frying pan. Cook the chapati for 1 minute until small bubbles appear.
6 Turn over and cook the other side for 1 minute.
7 Eat hot, usually with some spicy food.

Wholemeal bread rolls

Ingredients
200 g wholemeal flour
1 level teaspoon salt
1 sachet (15 g) fast acting yeast
1 teaspoon sugar
150 ml warm water

1 Place the flour, salt, yeast and sugar in a bowl and add warm water and mix to a dough.
2 Turn out and knead the dough on a floured work surface for 4–5 minutes until smooth and elastic.
3 Divide the dough into 6 equal pieces and shape into rolls.
4 Place on a greased baking tray, cover with greased paper and place to rise in a warm place for about 30 minutes.
5 Bake in a hot oven 220°C/Gas mark 7 for 20–25 minutes until light and crusty. The rolls should sound hollow when tapped.

Bread tasting panel

When the breads have cooked, form a **tasting panel** and try the results. Talk about how easy each bread was to make, how much they cost and how long they took to cook. Discuss how these two breads could be eaten with meals or snacks. You could compare the wholemeal rolls you made with some ready-made rolls.

Copy and fill in the chart below to show your results.

Bread tasting chart

	Chapatis	Wholemeal bread	Ready-made rolls
How long did it take to make?			
How easy was it to make?			
How long did it take to cook?			
How much did it cost?			
What did the bread look and taste like?			
What foods could you eat with this bread?			

Further work

Make a poster called 'Breads of the world'. Find out how the different breads are made and cooked. Why do you think different countries in the world prefer to make different types of bread? Explain why some people prefer to make their own bread, whilst others like to buy bread ready made.

Bread is one of the oldest **ready-made** foods and was discovered over 5000 years ago. This first bread was made by crushing the seeds of wild grasses to make flour. The flour was mixed with water to form a **dough**, which was dried in the sun. This bread was flat and hard like a large biscuit.

Later, people discovered that if the dough was left, it began to rise. Wild **yeasts** from the air had started to ferment the dough, producing bubbles of **carbon dioxide** gas which pushed up the mixture. When this dough was cooked on a hot flat pan, it made a lighter loaf. This was known as **leavened bread**.

For hundreds of years, white bread was popular with rich people, while poorer people ate brown, bran loaves. As **technology** improved the way flour was milled, white flour became cheaper and available for all. Today, white bread outsells all other types of bread. But as we try to eat more fibre as part of a healthy diet, so sales of wholemeal and brown bread are increasing.

Grinding flour

Stages in design and technology

- The **need** – customers want bread with more fibre.
- **Ideas** – find ways of adding extra fibre.
- **Outcome** – more wholemeal, brown and 'added fibre' bread is made.
- **Improvements** – recently more varieties of high fibre bread for sale.

Questions

1 How was the first bread made?
2 How were grains ground into flour?
3 What is leavened bread?
4 The graph shows the sales of white and wholemeal/brown bread in Britain over the last twenty years (bread consumption in the UK).
   (a) Which is the most popular type of bread eaten in Britain? Give a reason for its popularity.
   (b) Sales of which type of bread are
   (a) increasing
   (b) declining (going down)?
   Give a reason for these changes.
   (c) Which type of bread do you prefer and why?

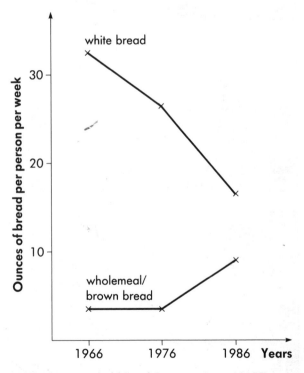

(Source – Household Food Consumption – MAFF)

Bread consumption in the UK

How is bread made in a modern, high technology bakery?

Stages:

1 Flour, yeast and water are mixed by a machine into a dough.
2 Dough is kneaded by a machine hook.
3 Machine weighs and divides dough into loaves.
4 Loaves are left on racks to prove for a fixed amount of time.
5 Loaves are baked in a computer controlled oven for a fixed time.
6 Freshly baked bread ready for sale – it may be sliced and wrapped.

To do

---

1 Compare the way bread is made in a kitchen to the way it is made in a modern high technology bakery. Use the wholemeal bread recipe on page 35 and the method used in a high technology bakery shown here. Draw up a chart like the one below and write in the different stages of breadmaking. The first stage has already been completed.

Chart to compare breadmaking

Bread made in a kitchen	Bread made in a high technology bakery
Ingredients weighed and mixed by a cook.	Machinery weighs and mixes the dough.

2 Many large supermarkets have in-store bakeries. Arrange a behind-the-scenes visit. Compare the way bread is made there to the high technology method shown in the drawing. Explain the differences.
3 Imagine that you work for the Bread Marketing Board and have been asked to invent a new bread. Adapt the wholemeal bread recipe on page 35, using extra ingredients such as peanuts, raisins, herbs or cheese.
Test out your recipe and write out exactly what ingredients you used. Design a name and a packet label for your new bread. Write out a list of ingredients for the label.

High technology bakery

Pasta is made from wheat flour, mixed with water then dried. In the past it was a way of keeping wheat through the winter months.

Who invented pasta?

Some say we were brought from China by the explorer Marco Polo....

But we were around before that

'Macaroni' is Sicilian for 'made into dough by force'.

Stages in design and technology

- The **need** – to keep wheat through winter and make a useful food.
- **Ideas** – Marco Polo saw the idea in China!
- **Outcome** – mix wheat with water, then dry it to make pasta.
- **Improvements** – today there are hundreds of shapes and flavours of pasta.

Today pasta has become very popular as ready to eat meals or snacks.

Flour and water are kneaded by machine into a dough.

↓

It is made into different flavours, shapes and sizes.

↓

The pasta is dried.

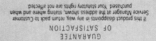

Heinz Spaghetti in tomato sauce

TO SERVE
Empty contents into a saucepan and stir gently while heating

MICROWAVES (650W)
Empty contents into a microwave dish, cover and heat for approximately 4 minutes stirring occasionally
Empty out unused contents, cover, keep cool

Made in England
H.J. HEINZ CO. LTD.
Hayes, Middx. UB4 8AL

e 425 g

FREE FROM ARTIFICIAL COLOUR AND PRESERVATIVE

Serving suggestion

5 000157 004444

INGREDIENTS
Tomatoes
Spaghetti (made from wheat and egg white)
Water, Sugar, Salt, Modified Cornflour, Cheese
Citric acid, Spices, Herbs

GUARANTEE
Price refunded, without affecting your statutory rights, if any Heinz variety fails to please

Heinz Spaghetti is made with fine quality ingredients to create a wholesome, nutritious and tasty food. Reflecting today's consumer tastes, the levels of added salt and sugar in our recipe are kept at the minimum possible without impairing your enjoyment of the traditional Heinz flavour. Heinz Spaghetti is entirely free from artificial colours and preservatives, the rich colour of the sauce coming only from the juicy red tomatoes.

NUTRITION INFORMATION

Typical Values	Amount Per 100g	Amount Per Serving (212g)
Energy	295 kJ/69 kcal	625 kJ/147 kcal
Protein	2.3g	4.9g
Carbohydrate	15.5g	32.9g
(of which sugars)	(5.0g)	(10.6g)
Fat	0.2g	0.4g
(of which saturates)	(trace)	(0.1g)
Sodium	0.4g	0.9g
Dietary Fibre	0.7g	1.5g

PASTA FOODS LIMITED, LONDON ROAD, ST. ALBANS, HERTS.
will absorb the liquid during cooking to give excellent results. Once opened the pasta should be sto...
or milk for white sauce). b) Always start with a layer of sauce. c) Make sure the final layer of lasagne is well...
Allow 12 sheets for a 23cm (9") square dish which will give 4-6 servings. a) Use a quarter more liquid in the...

HOW TO PREPARE RECORD LASAGNE

NO PRE-COOKING REQUIRED

Serving Suggestion:
NO SALT · NO PRESERVATIVES · NO ADDITIVES

To do

You could start a class project to show how popular pasta has become in recent years.

Make a collection of labels from ready to eat pasta meals. These can be from cans, packets or frozen foods. Use your labels and those shown on these pages to show how pasta is made into a variety of foods. You could design a chart like the one below to compare results.

Ready made meals with pasta

Name of meal	What pasta is used	How is it cooked?	Usefulness
Pasta pots	noodles		for people in a hurry

Talk about how the different types of pasta are packed and cooked. Why is pasta becoming such a popular food?

Home made pasta using a machine

In Italy this sort of machine may be used for making pasta at home. The picture shows three **moulds** (cutters) which can be used to make **noodles**, **spaghetti** or **macaroni**.

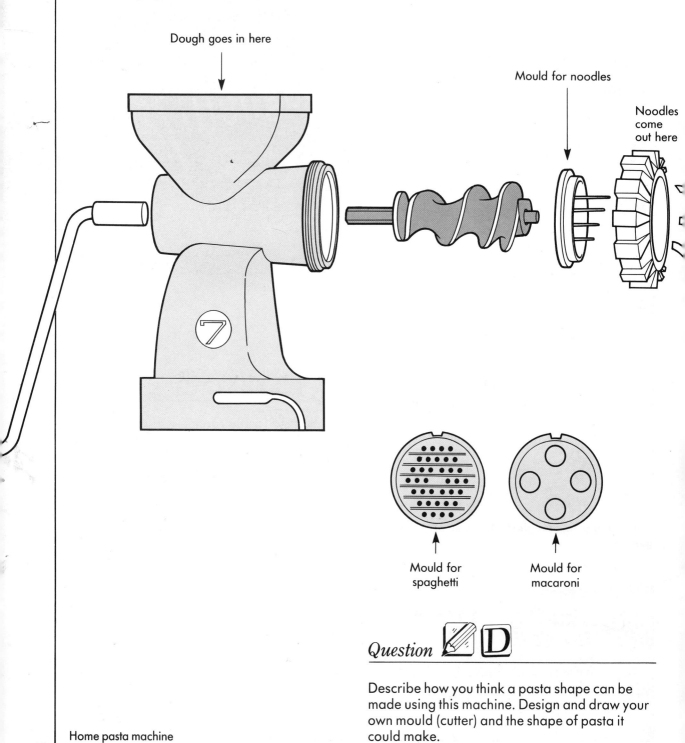

Dough goes in here

Mould for noodles

Noodles come out here

Mould for spaghetti

Mould for macaroni

Question D

Describe how you think a pasta shape can be made using this machine. Design and draw your own mould (cutter) and the shape of pasta it could make.

To do

Design and make a pasta shape.
Use the recipe for egg pasta then cook it and
serve with tomato sauce and grated cheese.

Egg Pasta

Ingredients
100 g strong plain flour
pinch of salt
1 teaspoon oil
2 teaspoons water
1 egg, size 2, beaten

Equipment
teaspoon
rolling pin
knife
bowl
fork
saucepan
colander

Method
1 Put the flour and salt in a bowl and mix in
the beaten egg, oil and water with your
hands.
2 Work and knead for 5 minutes to make a
smooth dough.
3 Half fill a large saucepan with water and
bring to the boil.
4 **Now design your own pasta shape!** Roll
out the dough very thinly and cut out your
design.
5 Cook your pasta for 3–5 minutes in boiling
water, or until it rises to the top of the
water.
6 Drain and serve hot with tomato sauce and
grated cheese.

When you have completed this task complete an
evaluation:

Evaluation of home-made pasta shape

● How successful was your pasta?
● What problems did you meet and how did
you solve them?
● What improvements could you make to
your design?

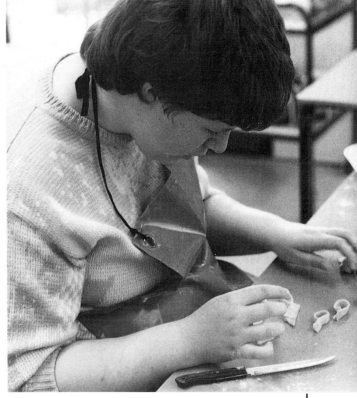

The inventor of 'fishini'

Fishini

Fishini pasta

Question

If you were a food maker, how could you make
large quantities of your pasta shapes? Describe
how the dough could be kneaded, shaped and
got ready for sale. What are the **constraints**
(things to think about) when making this food?

How cornflakes are made

Nearly one hundred years ago, two ready to eat **health foods** were invented which were easy to eat and digest. Dr Kellogg and his brother discovered how to make **cornflakes** – now the most popular breakfast cereal in the world. Mr Perky was the inventor of **Shredded Wheat**.

Look at the chart which shows the technology behind the way cornflakes are made in a factory.

1 HARVESTING
Ripened by over 140 days' sunshine. The maize which is to become corn flakes is gathered by a giant combine harvester.

2 SEAFORTH
The grain arrives by ship and is transferred by suction pipes to large storage silos.

The production of cornflakes

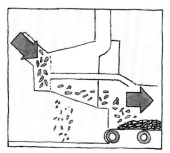

3 MILLING
The maize is milled into 'grits'.

4 FLAVOURING
Malt sugar and salt are blended according to a special recipe.

5 COOKING
The mixture is funnelled into giant cookers where it is sealed and rotated under steam pressure.

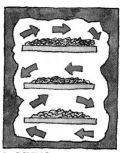

6 DRYING
The maize is dried in hot air currents and stored in tanks.

7 QUALITY ASSURANCE
Every stage in processing is carefully checked and controlled to maintain a high quality breakfast cereal.

8 FLAKING
Heavy flaking mill rollers press the maize into flakes.

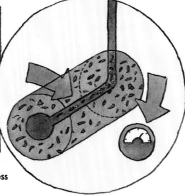

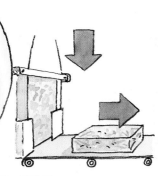

9 TOASTING
The flakes are tumble toasted in giant rotary ovens at high temperature.

10 FILLING
The toasted flakes flow from the oven to the filling machines and are automatically weighed in bags.

11 PACKING
Filled bags are passed along conveyors and packed into corn flake packets.

12 DISTRIBUTION
Boxes of corn flakes are sent by road night and day, all over the country.

Stages in design and technology

- The **need** – some of Dr Kellogg's patients need a tasty, low fat cereal food.
- **Ideas** – test out a recipe using maize, which is easy to digest.
- **Outcome** – the first cornflakes!
- **Improvements** – cornflakes made in a factory and other recipes invented.

Questions

Answer each of these questions in a sentence.

1 What cereal is used to make cornflakes?
2 In the cornflakes' factory where is the grain stored?
3 What flavours are added to the maize to make cornflakes?
4 After the maize has been cooked and dried, how is it made into flakes?
5 Copy the diagram in box 8 and label:
(a) maize, (b) rollers, (c) cornflakes, (d) conveyor belt.
6 Why does the factory check for quality?
7 Why do you think the flakes are tumble-toasted in a hot oven?
8 Why are the cornflakes, (a) sealed in bags, (b) packed in boxes?

To do

You have been asked to design a new breakfast cereal.
• Draw a design for the box with a name for your breakfast cereal.

Breakfast flake tasting

Collect some packets of different breakfast flakes which are made from maize and other cereals such as wheat or rice. Pour the cereals into bowls and then look at them carefully and taste them. Copy the chart below and fill in your comments. You can use the cereals to make chocolate crunchies.

Question

What is the difference between the breakfast cereal flakes?

Name of flake	What cereal is it made from?	Colour	Taste	Other comments
Team	Wheat, rice, Maize, bran			

Chocolate crunchies

Ingredients
50 g margarine
50 g brown sugar
2 tablespoons runny honey
1 tablespoon cocoa powder
75 g crunched-up breakfast cereal

Equipment
saucepan
wooden spoon
tablespoon
8 paper cases

Method
1 Heat the margarine, sugar and honey in the saucepan until the margarine melts and the mixture bubbles. Stir in the cocoa.
2 Add in the breakfast cereal and toss well.
3 Spoon into 8 paper cases and leave to cool.

For over half the world's population, rice is an important **staple food**. Rice was first discovered in the Far East and has been cultivated for nearly 5000 years. Today rice grows in over 100 different countries in both tropical and cooler climates.

How is rice prepared to make cooking easier?

Before it can be eaten, rice must be **prepared** or **processed** to remove the outside **husks** and make the rice easier to cook – a skill learnt several thousand years ago.

Rice is one of the oldest **ready-prepared foods**. When you buy it, all you need to do is cook it in hot water. There is no preparation and no waste.

The flow chart shows the stages in rice processing.

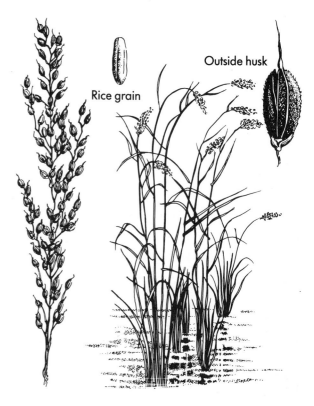

Rice grain

Outside husk

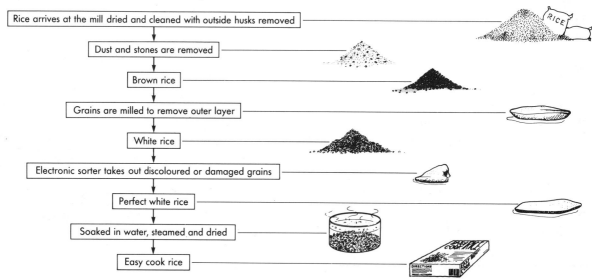

Rice arrives at the mill dried and cleaned with outside husks removed

Dust and stones are removed

Brown rice

Grains are milled to remove outer layer

White rice

Electronic sorter takes out discoloured or damaged grains

Perfect white rice

Soaked in water, steamed and dried

Easy cook rice

Questions

1 Why is rice a 'ready-prepared' food'?
2 Use the flow chart to explain the difference between brown rice, white rice and easy-cook rice.
3 Think of three other ready-prepared foods which have 'no preparation and no waste'.

Stages in design and technology

- The **need** – rice grains need to be made easy to eat.
- **Ideas** – find a way to remove the husk.
- **Outcome** – rice is milled and polished to white rice.
- **Improvements** – people want healthier brown rice, so technology changes.

Compare different types of rice

To do

Work in three groups – one to cook white rice, another brown rice and the last, easy-cook rice. Now form a **tasting panel** to try each kind of rice. Talk about the taste and texture of each rice. On a chart like the one below, write down the cost, how long each took to cook and the cooked weight.

Chart to compare different kinds of rice

Rice	Cost (per kilo)	Cooking time	Cooked weight	Tasting notes
White rice				
Brown rice				
Easy cook rice				

Key words to use
fluffy sticky nutty crunchy soft chewy

Rice salad

Ingredients
100 g rice from choice above
1 tomato cut into small pieces
25 g frozen sweetcorn
25 g frozen peas
small piece of cucumber, cut into cubes
salt and pepper

Equipment
large spoon
sieve
knife
chopping board

Method
1 Half fill a saucepan with water, and bring to the boil.
2 Add the rice, reboil, then simmer and cook until soft, but chewy. Note how long it takes each rice to cook.
3 Sieve the cooked rice and make a note of the weight of the cooked rice.
4 Mix the rice with the tomato, sweetcorn, peas, cucumber, salt and pepper and serve in a bowl.

From this investigation, explain the difference between the different kinds of rice.
- Why do you think they vary in price?
- Which is the best value for money and why?
- Which of the rices would you use as part of a healthy eating plan?

Give your reasons.

You could make them into a rice salad or choose a recipe yourselves.

Where does your milk come from?

Milk seller in the 19th century

For hundreds of years people around the world have milked cows, sheep, camels and even horses.

Cows in Britain were kept on **common land** or in fields, but as people began to live in towns and cities, the cows came too!

Milk was often dirty and people who drank it became ill. Milkmen and -women would deliver milk around the streets carrying two large tubs hanging from wooden yokes. This made them strong and muscular like the woman in the picture.

The change to clean milk

By the end of the 19th century changes began to happen – the **breeds** of cattle improved,

milking machinery was invented and milk was **delivered** by horse and cart.

The French scientist, **Louis Pasteur** proved that the bacteria which caused milk to go sour could be killed by heating. So, in the 1920s, machinery was designed for **pasteurization**, and milk became safer to drink.

Today, milk is packed in glass and plastic bottles and cardboard cartons. The bottles have specially coloured foil tops which show which method of heat treatment has been used, and also the fat content of milk.

Stages in design and technology

- The **need** – to provide clean healthy milk.
- **Ideas** – use Louis Pasteur's ideas and heat milk.
- **Outcome** – pasteurization is discovered.
- **Improvements** – later, other methods of heat treatment invented.

To do

As a class, make a collection of the different foil caps used for covering milk bottles and a variety of milk cartons. Find out about the different types of milk for sale and how each type has been treated.

Today there are many different types of milk for sale. They have been heat treated and processed in different ways to make them safer to drink and keep longer.

To do

Milk tasting panel

Form a **tasting panel**. Make a collection of milks which have been treated in different ways.

Draw up a chart to compare the price, colour and taste of each milk.

> **Key words to use**
> creamy fatty weak sugary boiled sweet tasteless thin

Use the milk to make a healthy milk shake. Here is a recipe.

Banana and oatmeal shake

Serves 2
Ingredients
300 ml milk
1 tablespoon oatmeal
½ banana
1 teaspoon runny honey

Method
1 Whizz all the ingredients in a liquidizer or processor for 30 seconds until frothy.
2 Pour into two glasses and serve with a spoon.

Questions

1 Why do you think it is necessary to heat treat milk these days?
2 Design and label a new container for milk. Explain why it is different.

Old-fashioned milkman

Puzzle

Years ago a milkman delivered milk to his customers. He would measure it out from large jugs. One day, he only took a 5 pint and a 3 pint jug on his rounds. How did he measure out 1 pint of milk for a customer without wasting any milk?

Answer

He filled up the 3 pint jug, poured the milk from it into the 5 pint jug, then filled up the 3 pint jug again. When he poured this milk into the 5 pint jug, he had 1 pint left for his customer!

Yoghurt

Yoghurt comes from **soured milk** and has been made for thousands of years by the people of Eastern Europe and Western Asia. They preserved their milk in this way but they had no real understanding of **biotechnology** and the processes involved.

The difference in **taste** and **texture** of the yoghurt from different countries depends on the type of milk used (such as cows', ewes', or goats') and how the yoghurt is made.

In Britain shops didn't sell much yoghurt until 30 years ago. **Food technologists** worked for many years to develop a choice of yoghurts which could be sold in the shops. They adapted old recipes and added new flavours. Now, in Britain, over 1 billion pots are sold each year. There are many types of yoghurt available – **natural** yoghurt, **fruit** yoghurt, **nut** yoghurt, **low fat** yoghurt and yoghurt **drinks**.

Yoghurt – what's it called?

Stages in design and technology

- The **need** – food makers want a new food made from milk.
- **Ideas** – copy yoghurt recipes from Eastern Europe.
- **Outcome** – factories start to make yoghurt.
- **Improvements** – a huge range of yoghurt for sale.

How yoghurt is made in the factory

Milk is treated to kill bacteria.

Put in large tanks and injected with bacteria "starter".

Lactobacillus bulgaricus.

Kept in a warm place. The bacteria in the "starter" grow quickly to turn the milk into yoghurt and makes it become thick and sour.

Cooled to stop bacteria from growing and making the yoghurt too sour.

Flavouring added.

Packaged and put into cold storage.

Streptococcus themophilus

The yoghurt process

48

Make your own yoghurt.

Home-made yoghurt

Ingredients
100 ml UHT milk
½ tablespoon milk powder
2 teaspoons natural yoghurt (starter)

Equipment
(This must be very clean)
jug
teaspoon
whisk
small saucepan or microwave oven
1 plastic cup or yoghurt carton
tin foil or cling film
paper for label
(thermometer – optional)

Method
1. Mix the milk powder with the UHT milk in a jug and stir well.
2. Warm the milk in a saucepan or microwave oven until it is just over blood heat (43°C). It will feel warm but not hot to touch.
3. Add yoghurt starter and whisk well.
4. Pour into plastic cup or clean yoghurt carton, cover with cling film or foil.
5. Leave on or near a radiator or other warm place (**incubator**) for 4–6 hours.
6. Cool by standing cup in a bowl of cold water.
7. Add flavouring and put in the fridge.

What flavours could you make?

Salad dressing — add 1 tablespoon chopped chives & salt and pepper.

Potato salad

Fruit yoghurt

Add 2 teaspoons fruit jam or chopped fruit.

Raita — to accompany a curry. Add 5 cm chopped cucumber and 1 tablespoon chopped mint.

What can you make from yoghurt?

Fruit yoghurt drink

Add fruit juice from a can of fruit and whisk well.

Add 1 tablespoon sugar, 300 ml water, 1 teaspoon lemon juice and whisk.

"Lassi" yoghurt sherbet drink.

Your own idea ?

What can you make from yoghurt?

Questions

1 What is done to the milk before it is made into yoghurt (see page 49)?
2 What happens to the bacteria 'starter' after it is added to warm milk?
3 Why must the yoghurt be kept in a cool place?
4 Use the yoghurt label below to answer the questions.
   (a) Is this a 'real fruit yoghurt'? Give one reason for your answer.
   (b) What are the first two ingredients added to this yoghurt. Why are they added?

To do

Ask some elderly people whether they eat yoghurt and when they remember eating their first yoghurt. Write down any other comments they make.

Design your own yoghurt label

Use the yoghurt label below to give you ideas. You could draw your label and stick it onto an empty yoghurt pot. Then display the work of the class.
1 Invent a **logo** with a **name** for your yoghurt.
2 Write a **description** for the flavour of your yoghurt.
3 What other information might you include?

NUTRITIONAL INFORMATION	
100g provides	
Energy	63 Kcal
	270 kJ
Protein	3.5g
Carbohydrate	13.1g
Fat	0.1g

ADDED INGREDIENTS: SUGAR, STRAWBERRIES, MODIFIED STARCH, STABILISERS E410, E412, E440, GELATINE, PRESERVATIVE E202, FLAVOURING. COLOUR E124.

125 g ℮

DO NOT FREEZE
KEEP REFRIGERATED BEFORE USE

ST IVEL LTD,
SWINDON, WILTS.

St Ivel prize STRAWBERRY VERY LOW FAT PASTEURISED YOGURT

St Ivel prize STRAWBERRY VERY LOW FAT PASTEURISED YOGURT WITH STRAWBERRIES

Prize yoghurt

Yoghurt flavours

A group of 30 pupils from Aspen House School were asked to name their favourite yoghurt flavours. Here are their answers in a bar chart.

Bar chart to show yoghurt flavours

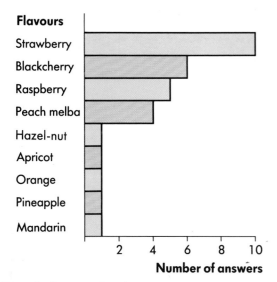

Favourite flavours of yoghurt

Survey

Plan and carry out a survey of about 30 people to find out:
1 How many times a week yoghurt is eaten by:
   (a) children (b) adults?
2 What is the most popular flavour of yoghurt with these people?
Present your results as a bar chart, pie chart or in another way. Use a **computer** to help.
Use your survey to answer these questions.
3 Who eats the most yoghurt – children or adults? Try to explain these results.
4 How did your results on the most popular flavours of yoghurt compare with the bar chart above?

Further work

Carry out a survey in the supermarket of:
(a) flavours of yoghurt for sale,
(b) types of yoghurt for sale.

Real fruit flavours

When you eat strawberry yoghurt you would expect it to contain real strawberries. But some yoghurts are '**fruit-flavour**' and do not contain any fruit. Real fruit yoghurts are made with 5% fruit by law and are allowed to have a picture of the fruit on the pot.

To do

Set up a **tasting panel** and find out if people can tell the difference between a real fruit yoghurt and a fruit-flavour yoghurt. Which do they prefer?
Use three different yoghurts:
(a) home-made yoghurt with added fruit,
(b) real fruit yoghurt,
(c) fruit-flavour yoghurt.

Tips

1 The fruit should be the same in all three yoghurts (e.g. strawberry).
2 The yoghurts should be placed in dishes and numbered so that the tasters do not know which is which from the labels.
3 Draw up a tasting chart like the one below, for the tasters to fill in.

Yoghurt	Which one is it?	Colour, texture, flavour
No 1 No 2 No 3		
Which one do you prefer? No 1 ☐ No 2 ☐ No 3 ☐		

Questions

1 Which yoghurt does the class prefer? – take a vote.
2 Explain your results. Can people tell the difference and which one did they prefer?

The first cheese

It is said that the first cheese was made about 4000 years ago by an Arab tradesman living in the desert. He milked his goat and carried the milk in a bag made from a sheep's stomach. After a long journey the man opened the bag and found the milk had separated into **curds** (solid) and **whey** (liquid).

A substance called **rennet** in the sheep's stomach and the warmth of the sun had turned the milk into **cheese**.

Before the introduction of **modern technology**, cheese was made in small farm dairies like the one in the picture. Rennet is added to the sour milk.

The picture shows a cheese press on the left and racks of cheeses maturing on the shelves.

The discovery of cheese

To do

Make your own cheese

Home-made cheese

Ingredients
125 ml milk
4–5 drips rennet
salt

Equipment
small saucepan
two clear glasses
spoon
15 cm square cheesecloth, muslin or 'J' cloth
elastic band

Method

1 Warm the milk in a saucepan over a very low heat. Test the temperature by putting a drop on your inner wrist or arm. It should feel the same temperature as your skin.
2 Pour the milk into one glass.
3 Add 4 – 5 drops of rennet to the milk.
4 Stir the milk a little.
5 Wait 20 minutes until it has separated. It is ready when you see a clear yellowish liquid (**whey**) covering the surface of the mix. Tip the glass. If the thickened milk (**curds**) breaks away from the side of the glass, it's ready.
6 Place the cloth over the top of the glass and secure firmly with the elastic band.

Making cheese at home

7 Turn the glass upside down over the empty glass. The whey will drain out.
8 Hold the curds in the cloth and squeeze out the rest of the whey into the glass.
9 Salt the curd and taste it.

Stages in design and technology

- The **need** – how to keep milk as a winter food.
- **Ideas** – make some cheese from sour milk.
- **Outcome** many recipes for soft and hard cheeses are invented.
- **Improvements** – a huge range of cheeses for sale.

Questions

1 What flavourings can you add to your home-made cheese besides salt?
2 Imagine yourself as the Arab tradesman or the dairy worker in the picture. Write a short story about your day and what you did. You might like to include some pictures.

Tasting panel

Taste and compare your cheese to shop-bought soft cheese.

Nomadic people who wandered around with herds of animals are supposed to have invented butter, made from the **cream of milk**, several thousand years ago. Butter will keep **fresh** longer than milk, and is useful for baking and frying foods.

In Britain, from the Middle Ages until butter was factory made, **dairy maids** often made the butter and cheese. These women had to be fit. In the north of England there was a tradition that the milkmaid had to lift the heavy wooden lid of the parish chest with one hand to show she was strong enough for the job!

A farm dairy, 1834

Look at the picture of the farm dairy. The milk is poured into bowls, the cream rises to the top and is made into butter by turning it in the two **churns** – one is by the dairy maid the other is by the door.

Today, cream is churned in large **stainless steel drums** until the butter separates out and buttermilk is drained off. Salt is added and the butter is cut and wrapped ready for sale.

To do

Make your own butter.

Make your own butter

You need

150 ml double cream   marble
jam jar with screw top lid   salt

Method

1 Shake the cream with the marble in a jam jar with screw top lid.
2 As the butter forms, drain off the buttermilk.
3 Add salt, if liked, for taste.

Questions

1 How is the way you made butter similar to the methods used by the dairy maid or factory?
2 Use other books to find out more details about how butter is made.
3 Write about 'A day in the life of...' using one of the people in the picture.

Foods like butter, vegetable oils and fat from meat and fish have been an important source of fat in our diet for thousands of years. We need fat for **energy** and to provide **vitamins A and D**. Technology has changed the sorts of fat we eat.

The invention of margarine

In the 18th century the population of Europe was increasing rapidly. All foods, including butter, were in short supply. By 1850 Napoleon III realized that if war broke out with Prussia, there would not be enough butter to feed his army. He asked his scientists for help.

The chemist, **Mège Mouriés**, designed a spread made from a mixture of **beef fat** and **whey** (skimmed milk). It looked white and pearly, so he called it margarine after the Greek word for pearl – *margaron*.

To do

Make your own margarine.

The first margarine probably didn't taste very nice. Try this old recipe for yourself.

Ingredients	Equipment
60 g lard	saucepan
20 ml skimmed milk	bowl
2 drops yellow colouring	wooden spoon
	mixer or food processor
¼ teaspoon salt	clean, empty yoghurt pot
20 ml vegetable oil	

Method

1 Melt the lard in a saucepan – do not overheat as it could catch fire. Let it cool for 3 – 4 minutes.
2 Mix the milk, food colouring and salt in a bowl then stir in the lard and oil. Whisk with a food mixer until it begins to set.
3 Spoon into a yoghurt pot and leave to set in the refrigerator.

Now taste your margarine. How does it compare with the margarines you can buy in the shop? Why is it different?

Margarine tasting panel

Questions

1 Investigate the different types of margarine for sale in the shops – for example, 'luxury soft margarine'. Find out what types of fat are used. What are the other ingredients?

2 Conduct a survey to find out if people prefer margarine or butter. Ask them to give their reasons for their answer. You could show your results as a bar chart or pie chart.

Use a computer to print out your results.

How were fizzy drinks invented?

In 1772 a British scientist discovered how to make **carbonated water** – that is, the fizz in fizzy drinks. He produced **carbon dioxide gas** by the chemical reaction of hydrochloric acid and marble, then added the gas to water by shaking them together in a sealed barrel. Water from the barrel bubbled and sparkled – he had started the fizzy drinks business!

In Britain chemists' shops began selling fizzy drinks to customers, adding flavoured fruit juices and sugar. Today we consume 3 billion litres of fizzy drinks a year!

The invention of fizzy drinks

Stages in design and technology

- The **need** – to tempt people to try new drinks.
- **Ideas** – a chemist discovers how to make water fizzy.
- **Outcome** – the start of the fizzy drink business.
- **Improvements** – healthier fizzy drinks and more variety?

To do

Make your own fizzy drink.

Orange fizz

You need
a glass
teaspoon
orange juice or strong orange squash
bicarbonate of soda or baking powder

Method
1 Pour the orange juice into the glass.
2 Stir in a teaspoonful of bicarbonate of soda.
  The orange fizzes and bubbles. Drink quickly before it goes flat!

Why does the orange fizz?

When **bicarbonate of soda** or **baking powder** is mixed with an **acid liquid** such as orange juice, a **chemical reaction** takes place. Carbon dioxide gas is given off and this gas makes the bubbles in your fizzy drink.

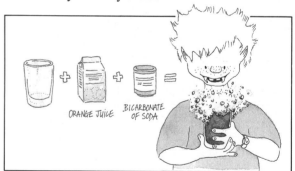

To do

What are the most popular fizzy drinks in Britain today?

Answer

lemon (lemonade, bitter lemon)	34%
cola	32%
tonic water	5%
orange	5%
shandy	5%
ginger	3%
others	16%

What are the most popular flavours of sparkling drinks for your class?

1 Conduct a survey. Ask each member of the class to list their top three favourite fizzy drinks. Make a tally chart to add up the results (see page 77).
Copy the chart and fill in a bar chart to compare fizzy drinks. Use a **computer** to help.
How did your results compare with the rest of Britain? Why do you think your results might be different?

How are soft drinks packaged for selling?

2 Visit your local food shop or supermarket and find out how the different drinks are packed. List the different sorts of packaging and beside each one give an example of the drink it contains. You could write: 'can – Pepsi Cola'.

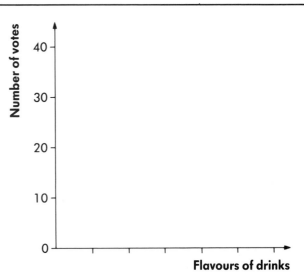

Bar chart to show our favourite drinks

3 In a group, make a collection of cans, bottles, foil pouches and drinks' cartons – this may be quite easy if you go around the school at break or lunchtime!

4 Each member of the group can now look carefully at one can, bottle,... Try to work out how it has been made. Make a drawing of the drink container. Now label the design to show how the can, bottle,... has been made. Show the **joins** and how it is **opened**.
Design your own drink container. Decide what sort of drink it will contain, draw a rough plan, invent a name then design a label (use other drinks to give you ideas). If you used old cans or cartons, you could stick on a label to show your design. Use a **computer** to help.

In the past, strange and sometimes dangerous ingredients were added to food – often to make more profit for the food seller.

In Britain, since we buy so much of our food from shops and supermarkets and not direct from the farmer, food needs to be **treated** to make it safe and pleasant to eat. Many foods contain additives, which are used to help food keep longer, and to change the **texture**, **flavour** and **colour**. **Food technology is about changing foods to suit our needs** – but do we need all these additives?

Some people are worried that we use too many **artificial additives** (made from chemicals) in our food. Food additives are tested by **food technologists**, and only after **much research** can they be used in food. The **E numbers** found on food labels mean that those additives have been passed as safe by the **European Community** (EC).

Look at the picture, called 'London improvements' from 1845.

sand is added to sugar

water is added to the milk

plaster of Paris (used for sculpture and moulds) is added to bread

vitriol (sulphuric acid) is added to beer!

London improvements

Questions

1 Why do you think people put those ingredients into the *four* foods?

2 Describe what you think might happen if you ate or drank these sorts of food.

3 Why do you think special food laws were introduced to control what is added to our food?

Stages in design and technology

- The **need** – how to keep food longer make it look and taste nice.
- **Ideas** – find some chemicals to preserve, flavour and colour.
- **Outcome** – food with additives.
- But the public wants fewer additives so food makers are trying out natural additives, or removing additives from some foods.

The photograph shows how different additives are used in foods.

REASONS FOR USE

Colours — to improve appearance
Preservatives — to increase shelf life
Emulsifiers/Stabilisers — to prevent ingredient separation
Flavourings — to add or intensify flavour
Antioxidants — to prevent rancidity or discolouration

Additives

Additives

Questions

1 Why do our foods contain additives? Copy the chart below and use the photograph to help fill in the boxes. One example has already been completed. You may need to use other books for information.

2 Use a dictionary if necessary to explain what is meant by the following phrases:
   (a) 'to increase shelf life',
   (b) 'to prevent ingredient separation',
   (c) 'to intensify flavour',
   (d) 'to prevent rancidity and discolouration'.

Additive chart

Additive group	Foods using this type of additive	What does this additive do?
Preservatives	Smoked ham	increases shelf life
antioxidants		
Colours		
emulsifiers/ Stabilisers		
flavourings		

Further work

As a class, design a display to show other members of the school how additives are used in **foods**. You could use **real packet labels** and look at the 'contents list'. Consider how useful additives can be, and also how difficult it would be to keep food without them. Perhaps you could prepare some foods which are additive free – this may be difficult, since bread, flour and margarine all contain them!

Food colours

Food makers think that people like food to have colour, so many **processed foods** contain **added colours**. Colours sometimes make you think of flavours. For example – green sweets might taste of mint.

Lemonade tasting panel

To do

What do colours mean to you? Try this simple experiment.

You need:
a large bottle of lemonade
some food colouring – red, green, yellow, blue, brown, orange,
some drinking glasses
teaspoon or a straw for each student

Method
1 Pour some lemonade into each glass. Mix a few drops of one of the food colourings into each glass. Leave one glass without any colouring.

2 Draw up a chart showing the different colours you have mixed.
3 Now write in what flavour you would expect if you tasted each drink.
4 Taste the coloured drinks.
5 What did you think about the taste and the colours?
6 Talk about how food is coloured. What colours are not often used? Why?

Looking at a label

1 The label for raspberry flavoured jelly **says no artificial colouring**. What natural colours have been used?
2 How has this jelly been flavoured and sweetened? Are any of those ingredients 'artificial'?
3 Discuss as a group the meaning of 'natural' and 'artificial' additives. Look at food labels and find out how food makers are changing what they put in their foods.

FOR BEST BEFORE SEE END FLAP

Raspberry Flavour Table Jelly

INGREDIENTS: Sugar, Invert Sugar Syrup, Glucose Syrup, Water, Gelatine, Natural Colours (Beetroot Extract, Annatto), Citric Acid, Flavouring, Acidity Regulator (Sodium Citrate), Acetic Acid, Raspberry Juice, Lemon Juice, Artificial Sweetener (Sodium Saccharin).

ROWNTREE'S JELLY

Raspberry Flavour

No Artificial Colouring

4¾ oz 135 g

Rowntree's jelly

Do additives matter?

Find out for yourselves!

To do

1 Work in groups and compare a home-made (school-made!) food with a ready-made one from a shop. Share tasks in the group. You could make Golden Rooty Soup and compare it with a similar dried or canned vegetable soup – check the ingredients list for additives!

Golden Rooty Soup
Serves 2–4

Ingredients
1 small onion, finely chopped
100 g swede, turnip or potato, peeled and grated
1 carrot, peeled and grated
300 ml water
salt and pepper

Equipment
chopping board
sharp knife
peeler
grater
saucepan with lid
measuring jug
wooden spoon
processor or liquidizer

Method
1 Prepare the vegetables and cook in a saucepan with the water until soft (15–20 minutes).
Season to taste.
2 You can blend the soup in a processor to make it smooth or serve it 'chunky'!

2 As you work, copy and complete the chart below.

	Golden rooty soup	Ready-made 1	Ready-made 2
additives	none		
cost			
cooking time			

3 Now taste and compare the different soups. Can you taste the additives in the ready-made soups? Which soup do you like best and why? Would you make the home-made soup if you were busy? Give your reasons.
4 Look at the soup labels. List the additives and use other books to find out what they are used for.
5 Use your investigation to explain why it is difficult to eat completely 'additive free' food.
6 You could make a display of your findings for the rest of the class.

Stages in design and technology
- The **problem** – people in Middle Ages need winter food.
- **Ideas** – why not try and dry some meat soup?
- **Result** – a gluey jelly which keeps through the winter.
- **Improvements** – better recipes!

Food technologists are constantly searching for new **sources** of food. **Quorn** is one of the latest foods which contain protein to be discovered and has taken 20 years to develop. Quorn contains **less fat** than meat or poultry and provides **dietary fibre**.

The growing of Quorn

1   The tiny plant that makes Quorn is a distant relative of the mushroom and grows naturally in soil.

2   The plant needs glucose, minerals, nitrogen and oxygen to grow. These ingredients are supplied to the **fermenter** where the plants grow rapidly.

3   After a few days, the Quorn is **heat treated** to stop it growing. Then the Quorn is made into thin, cream sheets with a wheaty taste.

4   Flavours and colours are mixed into the Quorn, then it is cut into slices or cubes.

5   Quorn can be used instead of meat for savoury dishes such as stews or curries.

Steps in making Quorn

Questions

1   Quorn is not grown in fields. Use the drawing above to explain where it grows and what it needs to grow.

2   How is this plant made into a food that looks like meat?

3   Why do you think people want to eat a food like Quorn?

TVP – textured vegetable protein

TVP is made after the oil has been removed from soya beans. Flavours are added and the mixture is made into 'chunks' or 'mince' for savoury meals.

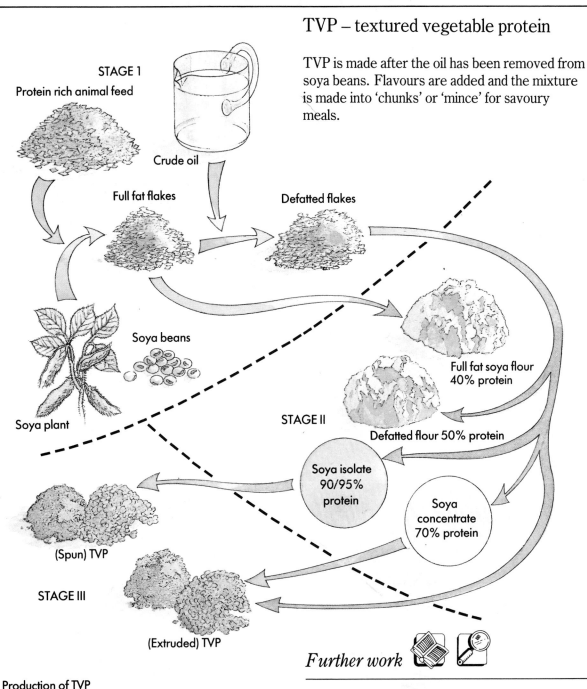

Production of TVP

STAGE 1
Protein rich animal feed

Crude oil

Full fat flakes

Defatted flakes

Soya plant

Soya beans

Full fat soya flour 40% protein

STAGE II

Defatted flour 50% protein

Soya isolate 90/95% protein

Soya concentrate 70% protein

(Spun) TVP

STAGE III

(Extruded) TVP

Stages in design and technology

- **The need** – to design a new food which costs less, yet looks like meat.
- **Ideas** – researchers and food technologists test out ideas.
- **Solutions** – TVP and Quorn in recent years – but more to come!

Further work

1 Visit your local food shop and make a list of as many foods as you can find which contain Quorn, TVP or hydrolysed vegetable protein. Compare your findings with others. What types of food use these new products? Talk about why food makers are using these new ingredients.

2 **Keeping up to date.** 'New' foods are being discovered and tested all the time. Look out for articles on 'new' foods in newspapers and magazines. Display these cuttings on a class notice board, and keep

From earliest times people have had to find ways to stop food from going bad. In summer there is plenty of food but in winter little grows, so to survive people learnt to **preserve** food.

What makes food go bad?

- Three microbes: **yeast**, **moulds**, **bacteria**, and **chemical enzymes**.

What do microbes and enzymes need to grow and spoil food?

- **Food, warmth** and **liquid**.

Early methods of preservation

Early people didn't know about microbes and enzymes, but they still discovered ways to preserve food.

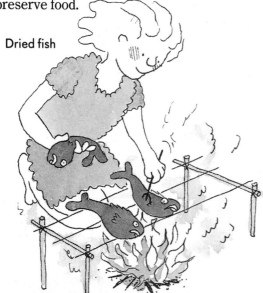

Dried fish

Stages in design and technology

- The **need** – to stop wet fish becoming smelly and tasting nasty.
- **Ideas** – 'I'll try and dry it out.'
- **Outcome** – 'I've invented dried fish for winter!'
- **Improvements** – 'now I'll try drying meat, vegetables . . .'

Dried food: fish, meat, fruit such as raisins, apricots, apples.

Why does it work? Most of the water is removed, so the **microbes** can't multiply and the **enzymes** can't react.

Dried raisins

Smoked and salted food: smoked meats, fish, salted herrings.

Why does it work? The chemicals in smoke and salt stop the food going bad.

Smoked meat

Pickling: pickled vegetables and fruit in vinegar.

Why does it work? Vinegar is too acid for **microbes** to multiply.

Pickling vegetables

Preservation

Food technology is all about changing food to suit our needs. To preserve food you must stop the microbes from multiplying by removing the conditions they need to grow – food, warmth and liquid. Early people discovered this form of technology by **trying out** different ideas. But at the same time they discovered that when you left some foods to spoil, you **created new foods** such as beer, cheese and yoghurt which were pleasant to eat. **More technology**!

Questions

1 Name *two* early methods of food preservation and explain why the food doesn't go bad.
2 Visit your local shop or supermarket, or look in the kitchen cupboards. List as many examples as possible of the following foods:

(a) dried, (b) smoked, (c) salted,
(d) pickled in vinegar.

Compare your list with those of the rest of the class. Make a chart to add up the number of foods prepared by each method then draw up a bar chart to show your results. Use a **computer** to help. Which method was the most popular? Can you explain this result? Talk about how food preservation has changed over the years, and why these 'old ways' are not so popular as modern methods of freezing or canning foods.

To do

Make some Pink Pickled Turnips – an old recipe from the Middle East.

Pink Pickled Turnips

Ingredients
450 g small white turnips, peeled and quartered
1 small raw beetroot, peeled and thinly sliced
300 ml warm water
150 ml white malt vinegar
2 teaspoons salt
1 tablespoon sugar

Equipment
jar
knife
chopping board
jug
teaspoon
tablespoon

made to my grandmother Fatima's recipe

Method
1 Put the turnip in a large glass jar, then place the beetroot on top.
2 Mix together the water, vinegar, salt and sugar and pour into the jar until the liquid reaches the top.
3 Cover with a lid and leave for one week. The beetroot colour turns the turnips a pale pink colour. Serve with salads and snack meals.

3 Use other recipe books to find ways of preserving foods at home. Test out these ideas – make chutneys, pickles, dried herbs and compare them with ready-made shop food.

Display as a spreadsheet.

How can low temperature help food to stay fresh longer? **Microbes** need **warmth** to grow, so if food is kept **cold**, their growth is slowed down. In cold climates in winter, people used ice to cool and freeze food for storage.

Cold storage

Supermarkets sell more and more chilled food, which is kept cool in special **chilled cabinets**. Many ready to eat meals are wrapped and chilled.

In large **cold storage warehouses**, food such as apples, pears, butter and cheese can be kept for up to ten months. Food from other countries often travels in **refrigerated ships**.

Frozen food

Today **freezing** is the most popular form of preservation in food factories and at home.

Most food is **quick frozen** since faster freezing results in smaller ice crystals forming. These cause less damage to the cells of food.

Invention of quick freezing

The Eskimos had long known that if they threw fish or caribou out onto the snow in the intense cold, it would freeze quickly. And it still tasted fresh and tender when it was cooked. An American scientist, **Clarence Birdseye**, invented a machine that could copy this method of quick freezing foods, the most popular method used for frozen food today.

Frozen

Small ice crystals

Cell wall

Large ice crystals

Quick freezing

Cell wall is still intact

Slow freezing

Cell wall has been ruptured by the large crystals

Thawed

Stages in design and technology

- The **need** – food that is frozen slowly is dry and tough when cooked. Need to find another way.
- **Ideas** – copy the Eskimos, but use modern freezing technology.
- **Outcome** – Clarence invents the first 'Plate Froster' for quick freezing. Today food from around the world is quick frozen.

To do

You can **slow freeze** fruit such as strawberries in the icebox of a refrigerator. When it is frozen, take it out and let it thaw. Now taste your result. Compare your 'slow frozen' food with the same type of bought 'quick frozen' food. Make a note of the differences in texture and taste.

Refrigerator

Chest freezer

Questions

Freezer ownership

Year	Percentage of households owning freezers
1970	4%
1972	8%
1975	23%
1978	37%
1979	41%
1980	46%
1985	71%
1986	74%
1987	76%

1 Make a list of *two* **frozen** foods which fit under the following headings:
Frozen fruit, Vegetables, Meats, Fish, Poultry, Ready meals.
Add a heading of your own.

2 Look at the chart which shows the percentages of households owning freezers. Why do you think the number of freezer owners is increasing?

3 Plan a supper for yourself and a friend which uses **only** frozen food. If there is time try out your idea.

4 Visit a supermarket and find out the sorts of food sold in chilled cabinets.

5 Ask some older people how they managed to keep food cool in the days before there were so many refrigerators and freezers.

Freezing and drying

In South America people have preserved potatoes for hundreds of years. Read the letter written by a young man from Bolivia.

Potato pickers in Bolivia

Questions

1 How do people in this village make Chuno – freeze dried potatoes? Write your answer in simple steps, e.g.:
   (1) Harvest potatoes,...
2 Why didn't British people freeze then dry foods in the past?

Hello, I'm Wilfredo Quispe.
I live in a village high in the mountains where the weather can get very cold. We knew how to preserve potatoes ages ago in Bolivia!
It's called "chuño" – freeze-dried potato. We watch the sky for the frost coming round about May, then harvest the potatoes. We leave them outside in little piles for five days in the hot sun during the day and the freezing air at night. Then we step on them with our bare feet to get rid of the skin and to press out any water. When they're ready we leave them in the sun for five more days to dry completely. Our "Chuño" is black and sometimes keeps for two years! When we want to eat it we have to add water and cook the potato for a long time to make it soft again.

To do

Divide into groups and discuss this question: Technology is about **solving problems** to sort out our **needs**. The villagers in Bolivia need food for the winter, so they dry their potato crop. How do they use what is around them to solve this problem?

For example, very hot days help to dry the potatoes.

How does this method of freezing then drying potatoes fit into the 'stages in design and technology'?

Copy the chart and fill in your own ideas.

Stages in design and technology

- The **need** –
- **Ideas** –
- **Outcome** –

New technologies for preserving food

Freeze drying

Dried food has been used for many years, but some foods on the supermarket shelves are **freeze dried** – foods such as coffee granules, dried vegetables and ready-to-eat dried meals. To **freeze dry** the food it is first frozen solid, then the **moisture** (liquid) is removed while it is still frozen.

This new technology is called **accelerated freeze drying**. Freeze dried foods keep their colour, texture and flavour better than other dried foods.

Irradiation

Special energy waves are passed through the food, killing off **microbes** and **unwanted pests**. Since the microbes which make food go bad are killed, irradiated food looks like fresh food but keeps longer. Fruit and vegetables don't go mouldy and potatoes don't start to sprout.

Irradiated food has been used for space travel and for hospital patients who need protection from infection.

In 1989 the government gave approval for food to be irradiated in the UK.

Energy waves pass through food and irradiate it

Potatoes stored for 9 months – the irradiated ones are on the right

Onions stored for 6 months – the irradiated ones are on the right

Further work

1 **Keep up to date**. Make a collection of cuttings from newspapers and magazines which describe modern methods of food preservation. Talk about why scientists are still trying to find new methods to keep food longer.

2 Find out more about **food irradiation**. You can contact the Ministry of Agriculture, Fisheries and Food for information.

Technology is about changing things to suit our **needs**. Throughout history, food for soldiers has always been a need. A well fed army fights well and conquers lands for their rulers.

Napoleon was desperate to find new ways to feed his huge armies – and so **canning** was invented. **Technology from need.**

To do

Look at the picture of Napoleon's soldiers, returning from winter battles. They don't look so well fed!
Imagine a day in the life of one of these soldiers. Write about your day as a soldier and how you managed to eat.

The history of canning

One of the most important steps in food technology was the discovery of canning.

History of canning

In 1795 the French Emperor Napoleon, worried about the difficulties of feeding his large armies, offered a reward for the invention of a practical method of preserving food.

About that time Nicholas Appert, a French chef, was preserving food by putting it in stoppered glass bottles which he heated in boiling water. In 1806 this method was tried by the French Navy, with meats, vegetables, fruit and milk, and it was successful.

Later Nicholas Appert was awarded 12,000 francs by the French for his food preserving method and his famous work on the subject was published in 1810. This was a very simple form of food preservation which was putting food into a container, sealing it, and heating it. The same basic principle is used in the canning process today.

Stages in design and technology

- The **need** – Napoleon needed food for his army in winter.
- **Ideas** – offer a prize for a new method of food preservation.
- **Outcome** – Nicholas Appert invented food sealed in glass bottles.
- **Improvements** – tin cans invented and first canning factory opened in London in 1810.

Today in Britain we eat 5½ billion cans of food a year!

Why is canning such a successful piece of **technology**?

- Canned food will keep for two years or more, in a dry cupboard.
- The food is ready to eat, there is no waste and it is easy to use.
- A wide range of healthy foods is packed in cans – fish, vegetables, fruit – without losing much food value.

Questions

1 How does canning help keep food longer?
2 Why do you think canning is 'successful technology'?

To do

1 Plan a meal, which comes entirely from cans, for yourself and a friend. Show how you could get this meal ready to eat in 15 minutes. Count down:
   zero
   1–2 minutes: open cans
   3 minutes: . . .
   If you have time, try to cook it, then test out your idea by eating it! Here is one meal.

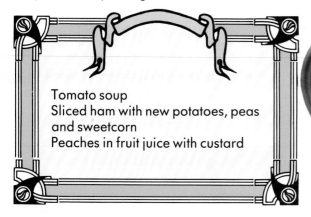

Tomato soup
Sliced ham with new potatoes, peas and sweetcorn
Peaches in fruit juice with custard

2 Talk about how the same meal could be made using only **fresh** ingredients. How long would it take to prepare? What problems might there be? Now write about the **advantages** (good points) of using canned foods.

Can designs

Cans come in a variety of shapes and sizes. Make a collection of cans yourself or use the picture to answer the question.

Why do you think cans have different designs? Think of reasons why the shapes and methods for opening cans have been chosen. Use the heading 'Can design' and write about your ideas. You can include drawings.

Technology is rapidly changing the way we do our shopping in Britain. Take food shopping for example. One hundred years ago, most food was sold from small grocers' shops. No-one is quite sure who invented the supermarket but in 1919 an American called Clarence Saunders changed his shop in Memphis Tennessee to self service. In those days, butter, biscuits and tea all had to be weighed and wrapped separately for each customer. Clarence decided to pack his sugar in pound bags, and tea in quarter pounds and let customers help themselves. The idea caught on. Customers saved shopping time and prices could be lower since Clarence bought cheaply from the wholesalers.

The picture below shows a grocer's shop in Britain around 1830. Notice the drawers and shelves for storing food, and the old weighing scales. Shopping has changed a lot since then.

A grocer's shop, 1830

To do

Use the picture to answer these questions.

1 Look at the chart below. Write in *five* ways in which shopping has changed since the 1830s. One example has already been completed. Add a sixth idea of your own.

2 Since this grocer's shop had no electricity:
   (a) what sort of lighting would be used?
   (b) how was food such as ham, cheese and butter kept cool?

Shopping in the 1830s	How has this changed in a supermarket today?
1 The grocer weighs out food for each customer.	Today food is prepacked and weighed ready to take away. Delicatessen counters weigh some food.
2 Cheese and ham are cut up at the shop counter.	
3 Food is stored in drawers and on shelves with a ladder for climbing.	
4 The grocer wraps everything in brown paper parcels.	
5 The bill is added on a piece of paper and the money kept in a drawer.	

Different shops

How is technology changing the **way we shop** and the **lifestyle** of the shopkeeper?

To do

Choose one of the shopping places in the picture above and answer the following questions:

1 How does the shopkeeper decide what new goods to order?
2 How does the shopkeeper order and collect these goods?
3 How is the food weighed and priced?
4 How is the bill worked out for the customers?
5 How do the customers take away their shopping?

You could write the answers, or try your hand at 'play acting'.

Play acting

In small groups of three or four people, act out the job of **shopper**, **shopkeeper** and **food maker**.

Choose the **type of shop** and a **food** for the shopper to buy; for example, a packet of cornflakes.

- How does the shopkeeper order and collect the food (cornflakes)?
- How does the food maker know how to pack and deliver the food?
- How does the shopper go about buying and paying for it?

Further work

Choose a shop in your area. Try to find out how the shopkeeper **orders**, **collects**, **weighs** and **prices** the food. What new **technology** is used to help? How is the **bill** worked out for each customer?

Selling around the world

People shop for food in different ways around the world. In Thailand, the man in the picture sells fruit from his bicycle. The mangoes, pineapples and watermelons are fresh and delicious, and his service speedy and polite.

Now talk about:
- where he gets his fruit from,
- how he pays for it,
- how it is priced and served to customers.

Question

Would this sort of shop do well in Britain? Give your reasons.

A fruit seller in Thailand

Shopping today

How is technology changing the way we shop today? **Computers** play an important role in today's shopping. They can:

- control and keep records of the amount of goods in a shop,
- read bar codes at the cash register,
- order more goods when necessary,
- keep a record of what is sold and when.

The picture shows a **computerized cash register** with a **laser scanner** connected to a **computer terminal**. How does this scanning system work?

1 The cashier passes items over the **checkout window** and the laser scanner reads the **bar code**, printed on nearly all items sold.

2 The scanner asks the computer for the **description** and **price** of the goods. So it might say 'JS BROWN SLICED 0.39' meaning 'a sliced brown loaf costing 39p'.

3 This information is relayed back to the checkout where it is displayed on the **customer display panel**.

4 Goods without a bar code and some fresh fruits and vegetables are priced and rung up by hand.

5 The laser scanner then produces an itemized receipt.

Computer checkout

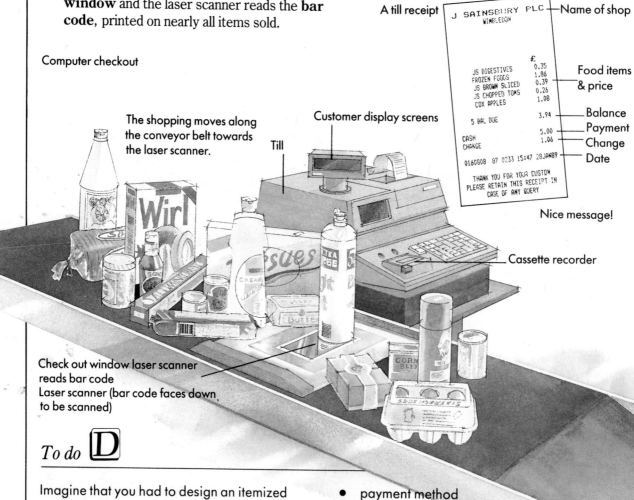

The shopping moves along the conveyor belt towards the laser scanner.

Till

Customer display screens

Check out window laser scanner reads bar code
Laser scanner (bar code faces down to be scanned)

A till receipt

J SAINSBURY PLC
WIMBLEDON

	£
JS DIGESTIVES	0.35
FROZEN FOODS	1.86
JS BROWN SLICED	0.39
JS CHOPPED TOMS	0.26
COX APPLES	1.08
5 BAL DUE	3.94
CASH	5.00
CHANGE	1.06

0160608 87 0233 15:47 28JAN89

THANK YOU FOR YOUR CUSTOM
PLEASE RETAIN THIS RECEIPT IN
CASE OF ANY QUERY

Name of shop
Food items & price
Balance
Payment
Change
Date
Nice message!
Cassette recorder

To do D

Imagine that you had to design an itemized receipt for the cash register of your own shop. Use the real example to help. Draw the receipt and write in the following details:

- name of shop
- food items and their price
- balance
- payment method
- change
- the date
- a nice message for your customers!

A computer programmer could program your cash tills from these details.

Bar codes

Many goods labelled in the shops are labelled with **bar codes** – series of bars and spaces which can be read using a **light pen**, a **laser gun** or a **laser scanner** linked to a cash register. All goods have their own bar codes which can be read quickly by computers. This helps businesses to **order** and **control** their stock easily. Most types of goods from food to books, fencing or even plants can carry bar codes.

How does the laser scanner 'read' a bar code?
- The **laser scanner** sends the bar code to an **electronic price file**.
- The **price** and **description** of the goods are sent back to the cash register's **display panel** and then printed on the **till receipt**.

How can bar codes help the shopper?
- Till receipts are more accurate and contain more details about what you have bought.
- The shop's computer can make sure that goods are not out of stock.
- If the shop wants to offer 'money off' bargains the computer can soon work these out.

Hand held scanners are sometimes used by shop assistants. You have probably seen shop assistants moving a small machine along packets or cans of food. These hand held scanners are able to read the bar codes on goods.

13-digit Bar code

5 012345 678900

2 Digits country of origin	5 Digits manufacturer number	5 Digits product code	Check digit
Internationally agreed	Allocated by ANA	Allocated by manufacturer	Allocated by a computer

Even pineapples have bar codes.

A hand-held scanner

Questions

1 How does a laser scanner read the information on the bar code of say, a can of peas?
2 How does this computer technology help:
   (a) the running of a large supermarket,
   (b) the shopper?

Further work

Visit a supermarket which uses a laser scanner at the cash register. Write about how it works and make a collection of some receipts. Watch a hand held scanner read the bar codes on shop goods. Find out how it works. Ask the shopkeeper how computer technology helps to run the shop.

Why package food?

Look at the photograph showing the spices, nuts and beans for sale in the spice bazaar in Istanbul. The food is displayed in hessian sacks and there are no prices or advertising signs. This food is not already packed, so the shopkeeper fills paper bags with the foods that his customers choose.

Questions

1 Why do you think the shopkeeper has chosen to sell food this way?
2 What are the problems with:
   (a) selling food from sacks,
   (b) weighing food for each customer into paper bags?
3 Why do you think many people like to buy food this way?

So why do we package food?

In poorer countries, less food is sold ready packed, but more food is wasted because the food goes rotten, insects can destroy it or it is damaged by poor packaging.

- Packets contain food so that it can be easily carried.
- They protect food from damage when it is carried around.
- Cans and special cartons preserve food so that it keeps longer.
- Packet labels describe food so that people know what is inside.

Can you think of any other reasons why we package food?

In the spice bazaar, Istanbul

Packaging

Stages in design and technology

- **The need** – find a way to carry eggs so that they don't break.
- **Ideas** – think of a package that will contain and protect them.
- **Outcome** –
- **Improvements** – what about the rubbish?

It's no good! Put these eggs in a packet.

To do

Visit a supermarket or look in your kitchen cupboard. Give *two* examples of how packets are used to:

- contain or hold food,
- protect food from damage,
- preserve food to help it keep longer,
- provide useful labels about the food and how to use it.

How is technology changing the way we package our food?

Technology is all about changing things to suit our needs. Here are reasons why our needs for food have changed in Britain.
- More women go out to work so meals need to be quickly prepared.
- More people own freezers and microwaves.
- We are eating more snacks and fast food.

Add some ideas of your own about how our needs for food are changing.

Why has packaging had to change?

If food is to be prepared quickly, food makers must do some of the work – for example, cutting up potatoes for frozen chips. New packaging has to be designed to meet the **needs** of ready to eat meals, frozen food, and packets which can cook in the microwave oven.

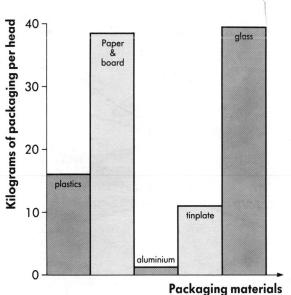

Use of packing materials in Europe

To do

1 Find out about materials used in packaging. Make a collection of different kinds of packaging.
Note You could just make a list, using examples from this book or by visiting a shop.

2 Talk about the different materials used in the packaging. Use your collection or list to fill in the chart below to show how the different materials are used. Keep a **tally** (count) of the number of times different materials are used.

Material used for packaging	Foods packed in this way	Tally count
Paper and cardboard		
tin cans		
aluminium foil dishes		
glass bottles		
Plastics – bags, bottles…		
total tally count		

3 Look at the bar chart showing the different packaging materials used in Europe. Draw up your own bar chart using the tally count from the packaging chart for your collection of packaging. You could use a **computer** for all of this work. How does your bar chart compare with the chart for Europe? Why do you think yours might be different?

Design brief D

Design a container to hold some sort of food. To follow a design brief, you must follow some **simple steps**. Then you can work in an organized way.

Stages in design and technology

- The **need** – what design to choose and make?
- **Ideas** – talk to people, look at other containers.
- **Outcome** – your own, specially designed container!
- **Improvements** – how could the way you work and the finished result be improved?

Food ideas

Step 1 Decide what your container will hold – try dry things for your first attempt, since wet, hot or heavy things are difficult to pack.

Pots of ideas

Step 2 Draw some rough sketches of your ideas.

Here are the rules!

8cm

m ← 2cm →

Step 3 Now plan an **accurate** drawing with **exact** measurements for the edges.

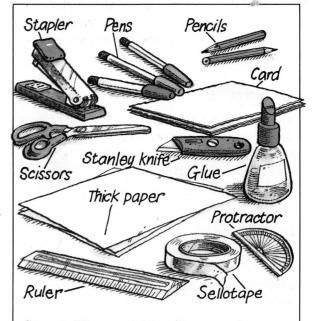

Stapler   Pens   Pencils   Card

Scissors   Stanley knife   Glue

Thick paper   Protractor

Ruler   Sellotape

Step 4 What materials will you use for your container? Cardboard, paper,... How will you stick it together? Make a list, then collect everything.

Step 5 Using coloured paper, felt tip pens and pencils, **draw a design** which you would like to use on your container. Try out two or three ideas and choose the best.

Step 6 Now get to work and make up your container. How will you fix on your design?

Step 7 When you have completed this **design brief**, with written work, plans and the finished container, think about how you could have **improved** your work, or how you **changed your ideas** as you worked. You may have found that glue wouldn't stick the box, so you had to choose something stronger.
(a) Were you pleased with your design?
(b) How could you improve?
(c) What parts did you find difficult?

Now try it out – fill it up!

Now present your work to a small group or your class. Explain what your container is for and how you planned and made it. Ask them for their opinions and ideas for improvement.

To do

As technology improves, we get more and more different kinds of packaging. But is technology a good thing?

In India, you can buy a takeaway meal, wrapped in a banana leaf. If you throw away this packaging it will rot and break down – it is **biodegradable**. The same is not true of a plastic hamburger carton.

Think about the **litter** and **pollution** problem in Britain.

Talk about the ways things could be improved.

This picture shows a farmhouse kitchen built in 1580.

Pendean farmhouse, 1580

Questions

1 Where did the farmer's wife store food such as meat, eggs, milk and fruit in this kitchen?

2 How did she keep foods like milk, butter and meat cool?

3 How did she cook: (a) meat, (b) vegetables, (c) bread in this kitchen?

4 Where did she wash up?

5 What happened to all the rubbish?

A modern kitchen

Now look at the picture of a kitchen with plenty of modern gadgets.

6 Compare the ways of storing food and keeping it cool in the *two* different kitchens. How would you cook meat, vegetables and bread in this modern kitchen? What happens to the washing up and the rubbish?

To do

Work in small groups and discuss how kitchens have changed over the years. Which kitchen would you prefer to work in? Give your reasons.

Cooking over a fire

Spit roasting

Controlled cooking

Look at the pictures which show how **technology** has **changed cooking** over the years.

Why do you think these changes have been made?

The technology of cookers

In the past, people **roasted** their food over **open fires**. Sometimes they put meat on a **spit** over the fire and turned it by hand to cook the meat all over. This meant that the cook had to sit there for a long time!

Later, some people used **dogs running in wheels** to turn the spit. This simple idea was the start of people using **technology** to control cookers.

A Victorian cooker

The Victorian cooker in the picture shows the idea of a cooker being shaped like a box to **trap the heat** inside. A kettle or pan could be boiled on the top and other foods such as bread could be cooked in the oven. There were no controls to make the oven hotter or cooler. How do you think the cook would make the oven get hotter?

Technology has improved cookers so that they now have **thermostats** and **automatic timers**, so you can set the exact temperature and cooking time.

To do

Investigate the 'high tech' extras which control the cookers in your Home Economics room or at home. Look carefully at the different parts and use a drawing to explain how the cooker works and how the heat is controlled.

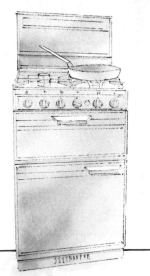
A modern cooker

Some cookers in the Home Economics room will have **automatic controls** so that you can prepare a meal then cook it when you are not there.

To do D

Work in a group and design a meal which can be cooked when you are out of the room. Here is one menu, but you could invent your own.

If possible, prepare the meal for cooking. If you are going to eat your meal at school, set the table. **Test out your result** – eat the meal!

Now complete an **appraisal sheet** like the one below. This will help you think about your work and how you could improve.

Menu

Gammon with tomatoes and mushrooms (top shelf)
Green beans or peas (middle shelf)
Garlic bread and hot fruit salad (bottom shelf)
Cook at Gas mark 5/Electric 190°C for 35–40 minutes.

Method

1 Find out how to use the automatic controls on on your cooker.
2 Share out the work between group members.
3 Read the recipes to make sure you know what to do.
4 Draw up a time plan to help organize your work.

Time	Person	What they are doing
11.00	everyone	set the automatic controls
11.05	Jo	green beans
11.10	Seema	garlic bread
	David	gammon

Appraisal sheet for my group

How easy was it to:

(a) set the oven ....

(b) share out the work ....

(c) draw up a time plan ....

(d) follow our plan and recipes ....

(e) work and help each other ....

The things we could do better next time were

....

The part we enjoyed most was

....

We thought the meal was

....

Stages in design and technology

- The **need** – to design a cooker which can heat up food when you are out.
- **Ideas** – find ways of turning the oven on by itself.
- **Outcome** – automatic cooker controls.
- **Improvements** – digital panels, computer programmed ovens.

Each of these recipes will serve four people.

Gammon with tomatoes and mushrooms

Ingredients
4 small thin, gammon steaks
1 medium onion, chopped
50 g mushrooms, sliced
2 tablespoons vegetable oil
25 g wholemeal flour
250 ml water
1 chicken stock cube
2 tablespoons tomato purée

Method
1 Put the gammon steaks in an ovenproof dish.
2 Cook the onion and mushrooms in a frying pan in the oil until soft.
3 Stir in the flour, add the water, stock cube, and tomato purée. Boil and stir until the sauce thickens.
4 Pour the sauce over the gammon steaks. Cook in the oven for 35 minutes.

Garlic bread

Ingredients
1 small French loaf
50 g margarine
2 cloves garlic, crushed

Method
1 Split the loaf in half lengthways.
2 mix together the margarine and garlic and spread over the cut surface of the bread. Sandwich the bread together.
3 Wrap up in foil and bake for 35 minutes.

Hot fruit salad

Ingredients
2 apples, sliced
2 oranges peeled and chopped
1 banana sliced
75 ml orange or apple juice
25 g flaked almonds

Method
1 Put the fruit and juice in an ovenproof dish and mix well.
2 Sprinkle with almonds, cover for 35 minutes.

Green beans or peas

Ingredients
500 g fresh green beans or frozen peas
10 g margarine

Method
1 Prepare the beans and place the beans or peas in a large piece of foil with the margarine.
2 Wrap up like a parcel, ready to cook for 35 minutes.

Equipment

knife	foil
chopping board	oven proof dishes
tablespoon	frying pan

The latest **technological development** to be used in many kitchens today is the microwave oven.

How were microwaves invented?
Scientists working on **radar**, which was used for tracking down enemy aircraft during the Second World War, discovered microwaves by accident. In 1945, Dr Percy Spencer realized that microwave energy produced heat, so he put a chocolate bar in front of the microwaves, and it melted!

The inventor of the microwave oven

Stages in design and technology

- The **need** – to discover more about radar.
- **Ideas** – scientists experiment and find out.
- **Outcome** – microwaves discovered as well! Today there are microwave ovens in 40% of kitchens.

How do microwaves cook the food?
- Microwave ovens have metal walls. Microwaves are reflected off metal, so they bounce off these walls towards the food.
- Water and fat in the food attract the microwaves which make the food molecules vibrate, causing **friction**, so the food gets hot and cooks.
- The microwaves pass through plates and dishes made of china, plastic or glass and enter the food.

What is friction?
You can produce friction by rubbing your hands together. Your hands gradually become warm. Just like the food in the microwave oven.

Why is a microwave oven different to an ordinary oven?
- Microwave ovens can be plugged into 13 amp sockets anywhere around the house. An ordinary oven usually needs a special fixing.
- Small portions of food cook very quickly and use less electricity. For example, a baked potato takes 1 hour to cook in an oven but 4–5 minutes in a microwave oven.
- A whole meal can be put on a plate then reheated from cold in the microwave oven, and still taste like it's just been cooked.

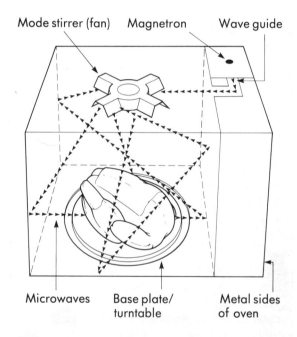

Mode stirrer (fan)   Magnetron   Wave guide

Microwaves   Base plate/ turntable   Metal sides of oven

Microwave oven

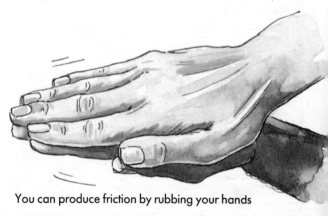

You can produce friction by rubbing your hands

But what are the problems with microwave ovens –
what can't they do?

Constraints

1 Food cooks so quickly that it can sometimes overcook.
2 Microwaves don't brown food – cooked chicken stays a pale cream colour. Newer ovens have grills and browning plates.
3 Some foods don't cook very well – for example, eggs boiled in their shells explode!
4 Metal dishes and equipment will damage the oven.

Recipes have to be **changed** if you are using a microwave. This recipe for cheesy scones is cooked in an ordinary oven. The cook has marked changes for cooking the scones in a microwave.

To do

Rewrite the recipe for use in a microwave oven, then test it to see if your version is correct.

Cheesy scones

Ingredients
225 g self-raising flour
25 g polyunsaturated margarine
50 g Cheddar cheese (grated)
5–7 tablespoons milk
beaten egg *leave out*

Equipment

bowl	cooling rack
spoon	grater
cutters	baking tray
tablespoon	

Method
1 Set the oven at 200°C/Gas mark 6. *leave out* Rub the margarine into the flour. Add the cheese and mix to a soft dough with milk.
2 Knead the dough on a floured surface then pat gently until it is 1.5 cm thick. Cut into 6–7 rounds using a cutter or glass. *leave out*
3 Brush the tops with beaten egg and arrange on baking tray. *plate turning ½ way*
4 Bake for 8–10 minutes until well risen and golden. *3–4 microwave at 100% (high)*
5 Cool on a wire cooling rack. *and brown under the grill.*
Allow to stand for 2 minutes

1 Visit your local electrical shop which sells microwave ovens, or use the microwave oven at school or home. Study an oven in detail and find out how it works. Describe any 'high tech' extras such as **turntables, temperature probes** and **memory programs.**
2 Conduct a survey of about ten people to find out more about microwave ovens and how they are used.
Try asking the following questions, and add some of your own.
(a) How many people own a microwave oven?
(b) How often do they use it?
(c) What do they use it for?
(d) What do they like and dislike about it?
Use a computer to design **spreadsheets** for your survey. When you have the results of your survey, use the **computer** to draw a **bar chart** or **pie chart** to display your work.

Questions

1 Why is a microwave oven useful for:
(a) a student living alone,
(b) a busy family who pop in and out for meals,
(c) an elderly person?
2 Imagine that you had to advise someone who wanted to buy a microwave oven. Describe how the oven works, then explain the good points and weak points of this kind of oven. You could present your work to the rest of the class.
3 Design a three course meal for one person which can be cooked **entirely** in a microwave oven. If possible, test out your idea.

In Victorian Britain during the 19th century, food was prepared in kitchens like the one in the picture. Since there was no electricity or gas, food was cooked in an oven heated by **wood** or **coal**. Water could be boiled on a **metal hotplate** on top of the stove. **Technological developments** have changed kitchens so we can prepare and cook food more quickly. For example, in the past, bread was toasted on a **toasting fork** in front of the kitchen fire. Today we might use a **toaster** or **grill**.

A Victorian kitchen

To do

1 Imagine that you had to prepare a breakfast in this kitchen. Your menu is fried bacon, sausages, eggs, tea and toast.
2 Copy the chart below and describe how you would cook breakfast in the Victorian kitchen.

Breakfast	What would you cook it in	How would you heat it up?
fried bacon, sausages, egg		
pot of tea		
toast		

3 How would you cook the same breakfast today?

Copy and fill in the chart below.

20th century breakfast	How would you cook it?
fried bacon, sausages, egg	
pot of tea	
toast	

Question

Compare the Victorian kitchen with your own kitchen. List five changes of equipment or cooking methods.

Equipment and gadgets

How has kitchen equipment changed and developed over the last 100 years? What modern equipment does the same job as some of the things in the Victorian kitchen?

To do

Copy and fill in the chart below. One example has already been completed.

Equipment chart

Victorian gadgets	What modern equipment does the same job?
bread knife knife copper kettle toasting fork hand food mincer wire whisk	similar bread knife, or electric knife

Are modern labour saving gadgets really worth it?

Questions

1 Use the equipment chart, and add ideas of your own, to list some modern kitchen gadgets. Explain how each piece of equipment might save you time and energy. Fill in a chart like the one below. One example has already been completed.

Piece of equipment	How does it save time and energy?
electric bread knife	cuts bread without much effort – but you can do the job without it!

2 Discuss with others the value of 'modern gadgets'. Do we really need them or are they just a luxury?

Technology has changed the **kinds of equipment** that we use in the kitchen. But has technology really made food preparation faster or better? Try this equipment investigation and find out for yourself.

Equipment investigation

To do

Work in pairs or groups and find out the best equipment for the following tasks.

Task	Equipment to test
peeling carrots	small knife, peeler, serrated knife, cook's knife
grating carrots	mouli grater, stand up grater, processor
chopping spring onions	small knife, cook's knife, autochop, processor

As you work, time each task exactly.

Prepare a carrot, spring onion and sesame seed salad.

Carrot, spring onion and sesame seed salad

Ingredients
carrot
spring onion
sesame seeds
oil
vinegar
a little made up mustard

Equipment
a watch with second hand or stopwatch
chopping board
2 bowls
spoon
kitchen paper
serving dish

Method
1 Peel the carrot. Put the peelings in the kitchen paper.
2 Grate the carrot finely.
3 Wash, top and tail the spring onion and chop finely.
4 Mix together the oil, vinegar and mustard in a small bowl.
5 In a larger bowl mix together the carrot, spring onion, 1 tablespoon sesame seeds and the dressing.

Now copy and fill in the chart below.

Task	Vegetable	Equipment used	Time	Comments	Mark out of 10
peeling	carrot				/10
grating	carrot				/10
chopping	spring onion				/10

Take a class vote to find out the most popular equipment for:
(a) peeling,
(b) grating vegetables,
(c) chopping vegetables.

Draw up a bar chart to show your results.

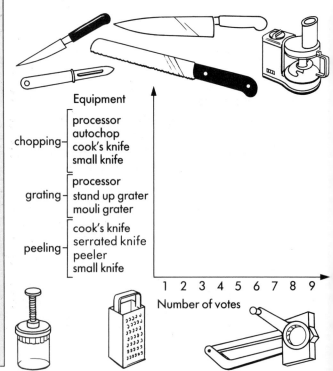

What about whisking egg whites?

There are several pieces of equipment which can be used to whisk egg whites. You could use anything from a **fork** to a **food processor**. But are they all useful? Find out for yourself.

To do

As a class, try out different pieces of equipment to whisk egg whites to use in apple meringue.

Choice of equipment	Time taken	How easy was the equipment to use?
fork		
wire whisk		
rotary whisk		
electric hand whisk		
large electric mixer		

Fill in your results on the chart. You will need to ask others for their results.

Appraisal

Which was the best piece of equipment for whisking egg white and why? Were all the results the same? Give reasons. Do you think it is worth buying each piece of equipment – why or why not?

Questions **D**

1 Invent a piece of equipment which is really useless at whisking egg whites. Draw and label your design. Explain why it won't work.
2 Now design an efficient piece of equipment for whisking egg whites. Draw and label it.

Apple meringue

Ingredients
1 cooking apple
1 tablespoon mixed dried fruit
little mixed spice

Equipment
knife
saucepan with lid
2 bowls
spoon
paper towel
something to whisk egg with
stopwatch or watch with second hand
ovenproof dish

Method

1 Set the oven at 190°C/Gas mark 5.
2 Peel, quarter then place the apple in a little water in a saucepan and cook for 5 – 10 minutes until soft. Stir in the dried fruit and mixed spice and leave to cool.
3 Separate the egg into yolk and white. Mix the yolk with the apple and place in an ovenproof dish.
4 Whisk the egg white until stiff, using the equipment of your choice. Time yourself exactly.
5 Fold the castor sugar into the stiff egg white and pile on top of the apple.
6 Bake in the oven for 15 minutes until crisp and golden.

Technology is about **changing things** in our surroundings to meet our **needs**. People around the world choose to make tools and cooking equipment from materials which are easy to find in their surroundings. So, in Britain Stone Age people used sharpened flint stones for chopping things and they cooked over open camp fires.

In hot countries the coconut palm provides coconut shells which can be used for pots, and the outside husk of the nut burns easily and makes good fires.

Stages in design and technology

- The **need** – we need some cooking equipment.
- **Ideas** – why not use some bamboo – but what could we make?
- **Outcome** – a sieve, steamer.
- **Improvements** – let's use other plants to make things.

Bamboo steamer

Coconut ladle

Gourd to carry water

Wooden board

To do

Form small groups and talk about how people, past and present, use the things around them to make tools and cooking equipment. Make a list of your ideas. You could display the work as a class poster with the title 'cooking equipment from around the world'.

Try not to think that one country is better than another. Technology is all about changing things to meet your needs, and if you have free bamboo to make a rice sieve then why spend money buying an expensive metal one? If in Britain we didn't have factories to make pots and pans, what would we use for cooking and eating?

One billion Chinese people eat food using **chopsticks** which can be made from wood, bone or plastic. Other countries may use chopsticks, knives, forks, spoons or, sometimes, fingers.

To do

Compare a pair of **chopsticks** with a **knife and fork**. Work in small groups and think about why some people choose chopsticks and others knives and forks.

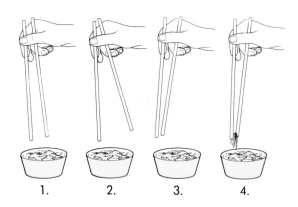

1.   2.   3.   4.

Which do you think is best? Some of the clues below may help.
- Which is the easiest to make?
- What are they made from?
- Which cost the most to make? Why?
- Which is the easiest to clean?
- Which is the easiest to use?

Test and **find out**!

Now talk about your findings and think about why people eat food with different equipment and in different ways. Choose one member of your group to present your ideas to the class.

Let's compare different kinds of cooking equipment. China has an enormous population and cooking fuel such as wood or coal is in short supply. Many Chinese people **stir fry** food very quickly in an iron curved pan called a **wok**. This method of cooking uses very little fuel. Compare the wok with a large saucepan.

To do

Prepare some stir-fried vegetables with noodles, or choose your own Chinese recipe. One group cooks in a wok, the other uses a large saucepan.

As you work, notice how quickly the wok or saucepan heats up and cooks food, how easy it is to toss and stir food, and whether the food sticks to or burns on the pan.

Try eating your meal with chopsticks.

Stir fried vegetables with noodles

Serves 2

Ingredients
100 g dried Chinese noodles
2 tablespoons vegetable oil
clove garlic, crushed
small piece fresh ginger, peeled and chopped
1 carrot, peeled and cut into thin strips
3 spring onions cut into strips
100 g beansprouts
2 tablespoons soy sauce

Equipment
chopping board
knife
wok or saucepan with lid
wooden spoon
serving dish

Method
1 Prepare the noodles according to packet instructions.
2 Heat the oil in the wok or saucepan, then add the garlic, ginger and carrot strips. Cook and stir with a wooden spoon for about 2 minutes.
3 Add the spring onions, beansprouts and precooked noodles. Stir and toss for a further minute, then mix in the soy sauce.
4 Cover with a lid and cook for 3 – 4 minutes until the meal is hot.

Questions

1 Write about your work with the wok and the saucepan. Compare the results you found. Which pan do you prefer for cooking?
2 Use other books to find out about how a wok can be used for frying and steaming food.

Glossary

Useful words to do with design and technology

Appraising After a piece of work is complete, you need to think about its value, how it could be improved and mistakes corrected.

Bar chart A way of comparing results by drawing a series of 'bars' on a graph either by hand or using a computer.

Bar code A system of small bars found on labels which can be scanned by laser beams to give information on the product.

Biodegradable Something which rots and breaks down in the soil.

Brainstorming A way to get a piece of work started. Everyone in the group thinks of as many ideas as possible. These can be written down in the form of a *spider diagram* which is a quick way of making notes.

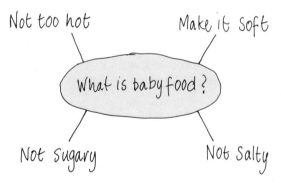

Spider diagram for brainstorming 'what is a babyfood?'

Design brief A task which has been given to design something.

Food technology Ways in which foods are changed to make other foods, safer food or preserved food.

Laser scanner A machine used to scan and read information on bar codes using laser beams.

Logo The design of the name or a product which is used on a label.

Market research In business, companies employ researchers to find things out for them before they make a new product. They may ask people in the street questions such as, 'how often do you go shopping?' to find out where to site a new shop.

Microbes Small, single celled organisms such as yeast, bacteria and moulds.

Nutritionist Person who works on the nutritional value of foods.

Pie chart Information is compared on a chart shaped like a round pie – sections are like slices.

Preservation Technology to stop microbes from growing and spoiling food.

Ready to eat food Food makers have prepared the food for simple heating or cooking (sometimes called *convenience food*).

Survey A way to find out things by asking people questions.

Tasting panel A group of people test some foods or drinks by tasting them and deciding which they like best.

This self assessment sheet is different from the others in the *Skills in Home Economics* series. This is because much of the work in this book involves some sort of 'design and make' task. This means there are more areas of work and skills to assess.

Fill in the chart when the task is completed.

You could use these symbols to describe how you worked, or design your own.

Symbols

1 I worked in a muddle and needed lots of help. I didn't finish the work properly.

2 My work was OK, but I could have done much better. I needed some help.

3 I did my best and finished the work. I feel pleased with myself and the rest of the group.

Assess yourself chart

	Symbols
Getting ideas Thinking about the task, finding things out, using books, asking people.	
Planning the work Sorting out what has to be done, writing it down.	
Practical work Testing out ideas – making things such as posters, adverts, testing recipes.	
Reporting and appraising Writing a report or talking about the task. Making changes.	
Group work Working with others in the class or group.	

The parts of this work which I found difficult were

....

....

I solved some problems by

....

I think my finished work was

....

Note

For shorter pieces of work which do not include all these areas for self assessment, you could design your own assessment chart.

The rice game

Start

Over half the rice eaten in Britain comes from the United States. Play the rice game and find out how rice grows, is harvested and prepared for sale. The American rice industry is thought to be the most **efficient** in the world since it uses **modern technological equipment** and **machinery**.

Rules

The aim – to plant, harvest and sell your rice crop.
Number of players – two to four.
You need – a dice and four counters.
How to play – place the counters on START, throw the dice and move the number shown on the dice. The winner is the player who reaches FINISH first, by throwing the **exact** number on the dice.

1. Farmer levels the land using modern machinery. Move forward 3.

2

3. Farmer cannot afford modern machinery, so his work slows down— Miss next go!

4

5. Farmer falls asleep whilst working – field uneven and cannot be flooded. Move back 3.

6

7. Farmer builds small dams to hold water— Move forward 3.

8. Dams have holes in them, so rebuild. Move back 2.

9. Dry weather. Not enough water for flooding— Miss a go!

10

11

12. The field is flooded ready for sowing. Move forward 2. →

13

14

15. Springtime planting – aeroplane used for sowing seeds by dropping onto water. Move forward 3.

16

17. Cannot afford to hire plane, so seeds are sown late. Miss a go!

18

19

20

21

22. Bad weather affects rice crop. Move back 2.

23. Insects eat rice crop. Go back to 14 and plant again.

95

4. Farmer sprays
gainst insects.
ove forward 3.
25
26. Rainy weather. Mould grows on rice. Move back 5.
27
28. After 100 days rice is ready. Throw again!
29
30. Farmer goes on holiday when rice is ready. Move back 3.
31. Farmer needs to organize harvest and book harvester. Miss a turn!
32. Rice is harvested by modern combine harvesters. Move forward 4.
33
34. Bad weather affects harvest. Miss a go!
35. Poor rice harvests due to pests and weather. Miss a go!
36
37. Rice is dried quickly for storage. Throw again!
8. Mice and rats eat the rice. Miss a go!
39
0. Farmer prepares
o meet buyer of
ice. Miss a go!
41. Price alert! Rice price is too low. Move back number thrown on dice.
££
42
43. Farmer looks for somewhere to store rice. Miss a go.
44. Lorry overturns carrying rice crop. Miss a turn.
45
46. Buyer cancels rice order. Go back to 40.
47
48. Rice prices drop and farmer goes bankrupt. Go back to START!
49
50. Farmer sells his rice at a good price and it is processed and packed ready for sale. Move to FINISH!
RICE
FINISH

Index

A

Accelerated freeze drying	69
Additives	58, 59, 60, 61
Advertisements	21
Apple crumble	27
Apple meringue	89
Artificial sweeteners	28
Aspartame	29
Assessment	93
Astronauts	14

B

Babies	18, 19, 20, 21
Bakery	37
Banana and oatmeal shake	47
Bar chart	92
Bar code	75, 92
Biodegradable	79, 92
Brainstroming	5, 92
Bran	32
Bread	26, 34, 35, 36, 37
Bread rolls	35
Breakfast cereal	42, 43
Butter	54

C

Canning	70, 71
Carrot and sesame seed salad	88
Chapatis	34
Cheese	52, 53
Cheesy scones	85
Chocolate crunchies	43
Cold storage	66
Computers	25, 74
Controlled cooking	82, 83
Constraints	5, 7, 20, 32, 41, 84

D

Design a package	78, 79
Design a pasta shape	41
Design a sandwich	10, 11
Design brief	79, 92
Designers	9
Dietary fibre	26, 27
Disabled	16, 17

E

E numbers	58
Equipment	17, 19, 88, 89

F

Fast food	12, 13
Fats	30, 31
Fizzy drinks	56
Flour	32, 33
Food colours	60, 61
Food technology	8, 12, 58, 65, 92
Freezing	66, 67, 68
Freeze dried potatoes	68

G

Gadgets	87
Glossary	92
Golden rooty soup	61

H

Healthy eating	22, 23, 24, 25
Home made cheese	53

I

Industrial revolution	32
Irradiation	69

K

Kitchens	80, 81

L

Laser scanner	74, 75, 92
Leavened bread	36
Logo	92

M

Margarine	55
Market research	8, 92
McDonalds	12
Microbes	66, 92
Microwaves	84, 85
Milk	46

N

New food	62, 63
Nutritionist	92

O

Orange fizz	56

P

Package	76, 77
Pasta	38, 39, 40, 41
Pasteurization	46
Pie chart	92
Pink pickled turnips	65
Play-acting	73
Polyunsaturated fatty acids	30
Preservation	64, 92

Q

Questionnaires	8
Quorn	62, 63

R

Research	10
Rice	44, 45
Rice game	94
Rice salad	45

S

Saccharin	29
Sandwich-design a	10, 11
Saturated fatty acid	30
Scientists	8
Scrambled eggs	13
Shopping	72, 73, 74, 75
Spaghetti bolognese	24
Stir fry	91
Sugar	28, 29
Survey	8, 51, 56, 92

T

Tasting panel	11, 35, 43, 45, 47, 51, 92
Toddlers	18, 19
TVP	62

V

Victorian kitchen	86, 87

W

Wok	91